The Rehnquist Court and Criminal Punishment

CURRENT ISSUES IN CRIMINAL JUSTICE
VOLUME 21
GARLAND REFERENCE LIBRARY OF SOCIAL SCIENCE
VOLUME 1137

Current Issues in Criminal Justice
Frank P. Williams III and Marilyn D. McShane
Series Editors

STRANGER VIOLENCE
A Theoretical Inquiry
by Marc Riedel

CRIMES OF STYLE
*Urban Graffiti and the
Politics of Criminality*
by Jeff Ferrell

UNDERSTANDING
CORPORATE CRIMINALITY
edited by Michael B. Blankenship

POLITICAL CRIME IN
CONTEMPORARY AMERICA
A Critical Approach
edited by Kenneth D. Tunnell

THE MANAGEMENT OF
CORRECTIONAL INSTITUTIONS
by Marilyn D. McShane
and Frank P. Williams III

INNOVATIVE TRENDS AND
SPECIALIZED STRATEGIES IN
COMMUNITY-BASED CORRECTIONS
edited by Charles B. Fields

THE WINDS OF INJUSTICE
*American Indians and the
U.S. Government*
by Laurence French

ALTERED STATES OF MIND
Critical Observations of the Drug War
edited by Peter Kraska

CONTROLLING STATE CRIME
An Introduction
edited by Jeffrey Ian Ross

MEDIA, PROCESS, AND THE SOCIAL
CONSTRUCTION OF CRIME
Studies in Newsmaking Criminology
edited by Gregg Barak

ACADEMIC PROFESSIONALISM
IN LAW ENFORCEMENT
by Bernadette Jones Palombo

AFRICAN-AMERICAN
ORGANIZED CRIME
A Social History
by Rufus Schatzberg and Robert J. Kelly

AFRICAN AMERICANS AND THE
CRIMINAL JUSTICE SYSTEM
by Marvin D. Free, Jr.

POLICING CHANGE, CHANGING POLICE
International Perspectives
edited by Otwin Marenin

ENVIRONMENTAL CRIME
AND CRIMINALITY
Theoretical and Practical Issues
edited by Sally M. Edwards,
Terry D. Edwards, and Charles B. Fields

THE CONTOURS OF
PSYCHIATRIC JUSTICE
*A Postmodern Critique of Mental
Illness, Criminal Insanity, and the Law*
by Bruce A. Arrigo

THE SOUTHERN SUBCULTURE
OF DRINKING AND DRIVING
*A Generalized Deviance Model
for the Southern White Male*
by Julian B. Roebuck and
Komanduri S. Murty

COMPARATIVE DELINQUENCY
India and the United States
by Clayton A. Hartjen and Sesha Kethineni

RACE, GENDER, AND CLASS
IN CRIMINOLOGY
The Intersection
edited by Martin D. Schwartz
and Dragan Milovanovic

THE REHNQUIST COURT
AND CRIMINAL PUNISHMENT
by Christopher E. Smith

POSTMODERN CRIMINOLOGY
by Dragan Milovanovic

THE REHNQUIST COURT AND CRIMINAL PUNISHMENT

CHRISTOPHER E. SMITH

GARLAND PUBLISHING, INC.
NEW YORK AND LONDON
1997

Library of Congress Cataloging-in-Publication Data

Smith, Christopher E.
    The Rehnquist court and criminal punishment / by Christopher E.
Smith.
        p.   cm. — (Garland reference library of social science ; v. 1137.
Current issues in criminal justice ; v. 21)
    Includes bibliographical references and index.
    ISBN 0-8153-2573-8 (alk. paper)
    1. Punishment—United States—History.   2. United States. Supreme
Court—History.   I. Title.   II. Series: Garland reference library of social
science ; v. 1137.   III. Series: Garland reference library of social science.
Current issues in criminal justice ; v. 21.
    KF9225.S64   1997
    345.73'077—dc21   97-10778
                                                                        CIP

Printed on acid-free, 250-year-life paper
Manufactured in the United States of America

For George F. Cole

Teacher, Mentor, Friend

Series Editor's Foreword

There could not be a more opportune time for Christopher E. Smith's book on the Supreme Court and punishment. In an organized and easily readable format, Smith takes us through the sentencing and incarceration issues that have been so controversial and yet, in a twist of irony, so relatively unchanged over the years. Although specific procedures and policies may evolve, the general nature and tendencies of punishment appear to remain somewhat stable in our society. This informative and insightful document attests to a legacy of excess and paradox.

It is ironic indeed that the Court, the institution set up to insure that the government does not trample on the rights of individual citizens, is criticized for giving those citizens too many rights. When the court does what it was engineered to do—insure a system of checks and balances and provide guidance for Constitutional compliance—it is chastized and ridiculed by an angry citizenry and media. Although the Supreme Court is theoretically a reflection of the values and standards of contemporary society, it seems to satisfy few.

While police actions and trial proceedings appear to generate public debate and media attention, the inner workings of the prison are still somewhat closed and secretive. In discussions of basic rights and protections, the Eighth Amendment has become the "other" amendment—less analyzed and theorized about than the others. Professor Smith's work begins to rectify this slight. *The Rehnquist Court and Criminal Punishment* provides a much needed commentary about contemporary punishment. Smith wisely leaves the reader to draw any conclusions about justice in the criminal justice system.

Marilyn D. McShane
Frank P. Williams III

Contents

Preface   ix

1 The Rehnquist Court and Criminal Punishment   3

2 Implementing Punishment: Excessive Sentences
and Prison Conditions   39

3 The Ultimate Punishment: Discretion and
Discrimination in the Death Penalty   71

4 Access to Justice on the Road to Punishment   101

5 Conclusion   127

References   135

Cases Cited   147

Index   151

Preface

Crime continues to be a problem that captures the attention of the news media, researchers, government officials, and the American public. It simultaneously inspires fear in the public, fear that is fed by the messages we receive from the media and politicians. Our inability to "stop" crime is not surprising in light of the myriad and diverse causes of crime and motivations of lawbreakers. Competing politicians are not deterred by our lack of success as they perpetually promise the public that they, and not their political opponents, know best how to handle the crime problem. Of course, because crime is not easily controlled, elected officials must find actions that are actually within their powers and exploit those actions to demonstrate their effective leadership against crime and criminals. The element of criminal justice most readily grasped and shaped by politicians is the definition of punishment for criminal offenses. They cannot control crime, but they can impose severe punishments on those individuals who are caught and convicted. In particular, the highly touted "War on Drugs" has not stopped drug abuse, but it has contributed to a tripling of American prison populations during the past fifteen years even as crime rates for many violent offenses have declined.

The recent emphasis on long prison terms, despite their questionable efficacy, raises many questions about the impact of increasingly punitive policies. Many of these questions concern larger expenditures: Will state governments threaten their own financial health by continuing to build expensive new prisons? Will the public be willing to pay additional taxes to incarcerate larger numbers of convicted offenders without demonstrable evidence that this costly incarceration is, in fact, reducing crime in a cost effective manner? Will citizens sacrifice government support for education, roads, and other services in order to spend more money on criminal justice institutions? These fiscal policy issues will be determined by the interactions of voters, legislatures, and governors.

There is another set of questions, however, that draws the judiciary into the fray and that affects the constitutional rights and liberties of citizens drawn into the justice system: Are the constitutional rights of defendants adequately protected in a punitive political environment? Do convicted offenders receive proper Eighth Amendment protection as states handle larger and larger numbers of incarcerated offenders? We often think of the U.S. Supreme Court as bearing primary responsibility for ensuring that these questions are addressed. Indeed, the Warren Court justices (1953-1969) strongly established the Court's image as the institution willing and able to clash with both other governmental branches and public opinion in upholding an obligation to make constitutional rights a paramount priority. In recent years, however, the high court's composition has shifted in a conservative direction. New appointees have brought to the Court different conceptions about the judiciary's proper role in the governing system and the Court's responsibilities for safeguarding the rights of individuals within the criminal justice system. The changes in judicial decision making by the Rehnquist Court justices (post-1986) in particular have significantly affected the treatment of defendants and convicted offenders. This book seeks to describe and analyze the Rehnquist Court's impact by focusing on the implications of Supreme Court decisions affecting criminal punishment.

The realm of criminal punishment raises most clearly the starkest issues of judicial responsibility and societal commitment to the concept of constitutional rights. Criminal punishment issues involve constitutional claims by the weakest and most despised of political minorities--one that has earned its despised status by violating the highly valued societal rules designed to, among other things, preserve order and prevent chaos. In the twentieth century, political minorities have looked to the Supreme Court for protection because the Court's justices, as federal judicial officers with protected tenure, presumably have the necessary insulation from politics to "do the right thing," even if that "thing" is unpopular. In the case of criminal defendants, and especially convicted offenders, the human beings beneath the black judicial robes must struggle with their own lack of sympathy for or aversion to these citizens who seek the Constitution's protections.

Criminal punishment issues also raise the most important human implications in a society that values life and liberty. The Supreme

Court is forced to develop rules to determine who will live and who will die, especially as capital punishment remains popular with politicians and policymakers. The Court must also consider the conditions under which other offenders will be incarcerated. These conditions define the environment that will affect the daily lives of many prisoners for decades and decades. How will "humane" standards be defined for the treatment of those citizens whom society despises? These issues are not easily addressed, yet in many respects, they may provide the most fundamental tests of the American governing system's genuine commitment to the idealistic principles articulated in the Bill of Rights.

I owe many debts to people who have contributed to my education and thinking about the issues discussed in this book. I am solely responsible for the book's contents and conclusions, yet many people have played a role in the development of this book. My interest in the book's subject matter is fueled, in part, by my memories of personal acquaintances who have spent time in prisons and jails or are currently serving sentences--students in the classes I taught at prisons in Washington and Connecticut, old schoolmates and Little League teammates, and others whom I have encountered in other contexts. Although they are not necessarily friends of mine nor people with whom I still have contact, they provide a human "face" for a group that society can easily--and understandably--dismiss as criminals unworthy of any constitutional protection.

In the academic world, I am grateful to my frequent partner, Thomas Hensley of Kent State University, who continues to enhance my knowledge about the Supreme Court as we undertake projects together. He also generously organized the data from the Supreme Court Judicial Database which provides the basis for the comparisons in Table 1. Similar credit is due to my other important scholarly partners, Joyce Baugh of Central Michigan University and David Schultz of the University of Wisconsin/River Falls, who work with me on Supreme Court-related topics. My former students, soon-to-be-professors in their own right, Scott Patrick Johnson of Kent State University and Avis Alexandria Jones of the University of Maryland, deserve acknowledgement for contributing to my early work on topics discussed in the book. My current student, Donald Kall Loper of Michigan State University, has been similarly helpful. Several additional scholars deserve thanks for sharing materials or providing encouragement: Neil Cohen, University of Tennessee College of Law; Samuel Gross, University of Michigan School of Law; Larry Yackle,

Boston University School of Law; the Hon. Julian Cook, Chief Judge, U.S. District Court for the Eastern District of Michigan; Mark Kende, Thomas Cooley Law School. I am indebted to Merry Morash and my other faculty colleagues in the School of Criminal Justice at Michigan State University for providing a supportive environment for research and writing. I am especially grateful to Beverley Bockes for providing me with invaluable technical resources and assistance.

I owe a special debt to George F. Cole of the University of Connecticut, to whom this book is dedicated, for introducing me to the study of criminal justice and for continuing to provide essential advice and encouragement.

As with all of my books, my wife Charlotte and my children, Alicia and Eric, deserve special credit for their patience and support.

THE REHNQUIST COURT
AND CRIMINAL PUNISHMENT

CHAPTER 1

The Rehnquist Court and Criminal Punishment

The distinguishing feature of criminal law is punishment. Among the various rules and norms that guide behavior in American society, criminal laws are unique because the government, through legislative enactments, has consciously decided to apply its strongest coercive powers to punish those who violate this special set of rules. Individuals convicted of violating criminal laws may receive a variety of punishments, including fines and probation. When convicted of serious crimes, offenders face the prospect of losing their liberty, the very thing which Americans historically, from Patrick Henry to today, have claimed to value most. Convicted offenders lose their liberty through imprisonment and, in many states, through the forfeiture of their very lives by execution.

The U.S. Constitution does not treat lightly this possibility of losing liberty or even one's life as the punishment for criminal offenses. The original Constitution demonstrated its concern that the government not possess the power to deprive people of their liberty without just cause. The Constitution explicitly preserved "[t]he privilege of the writ of *habeas corpus*" (Art. I, sec. 9), the legal action through which detained individuals can challenge the basis for their confinement. Several constitutional amendments reinforced this concern by establishing rights to "a speedy and public trial, by an impartial jury of the State and district wherein the crime shall have been committed,...be confronted by witnesses against him [or her];...and to have the assistance of counsel for his [or her] defense" (Sixth Amendment). Through these and other constitutional provisions, the framers of the Constitution and the Bill of Rights sought to go beyond mere symbolic statements about liberty as a treasured value or about skepticism of governmental power.

Instead, they attempted to provide procedural mechanisms that would protect Americans against unjust deprivations of liberty.

Although the Constitution provides an authoritative forum for the expression of national values and policy preferences, the words of the governing document are not self-effectuating. The history of American civil liberties demonstrates that the words of the Constitution have not provided clear, uncontested meanings conducive to easy implementation by authoritative officials (Abraham 1988). Instead, the interpretation and implementation of policies and procedures to protect constitutional values have changed in conjunction with evolving societal attitudes, new historical developments, and personnel changes affecting authoritative institutions. In the realm of criminal justice, actions by judges, prosecutors, legislators, and executive officials have created and altered the procedures and policies that determine the identification, apprehension, processing, conviction, and punishment of criminal offenders (Bodenhamer 1992).

Among the authoritative actors and institutions that influence criminal justice, the U.S. Supreme Court stands out as the institution with special responsibilities for interpreting and applying the provisions of the U.S. Constitution. The Supreme Court "stands at the literal and symbolic pinnacle of the American court system[s]" (Smith 1993b, 249). As such, its decisions can affect the processing of criminal defendants and the preservation or deprivation of their liberty in all levels of courts throughout the entire country. The Constitution itself does not guarantee that the Supreme Court will have exclusive control over the definition and protection of liberty. Indeed, judge-scholars Robert Bork (1990, 4-5) and Antonin Scalia (Smith 1990a, 793), among others, have argued that the definition and protection of liberty rests on the structure of the governing system rather than in the hands of the Supreme Court or any other governing institution. However, the nation's highest court has assumed a particularly important role with respect to constitutional interpretation and the definition and adaptation of constitutional provisions affecting rights and liberties.

According to John Brigham (1987, 51), the Supreme Court's "justices have solidified [their interpretive powers] by careful manipulation of authority given them and [through] the mythology surrounding law." Over the course of American history, the Supreme Court has established itself as the primary, authoritative interpreter of the Constitution. In Robert McCloskey's (1994, 12) words,

> The Court's claim on the American mind derives
> from the myth of an impartial, judicious tribunal
> whose duty it is to preserve our sense of continuity

with fundamental law. Because that law was initially stated in ambiguous terms, it has been the duty of the Court to make "policy decisions" about it, that is, to decide what it means in the circumstances existing when the question is presented.

Although government officials, including those in the criminal justice process, do not always obey the Supreme Court's decisions (Johnson and Canon 1984), the Court's interpretations of the Constitution are especially important and influential in defining the procedures that will determine the fate of individuals' liberty.

In cases affecting criminal justice officials and institutions, as in cases concerning other issues, the Supreme Court usually becomes involved in policy making in response to individuals' assertions that their constitutional rights have been violated by governmental policies or practices. For example, a defendant may assert that his or her Fourth Amendment right to be free from "unreasonable searches and seizures" was violated by the actions of law enforcement officials in conducting the search of a house or a car. Alternatively, a convicted offender may assert that his or her Eighth Amendment right against "cruel and unusual punishments" is violated by the overcrowded conditions within a correctional institution. By interpreting the Bill of Rights and other provisions of the Constitution, the Supreme Court creates rules that constrain the choices and guide the behavior of governmental officials in the criminal justice system. These judicially created guidelines touch nearly every aspect of the criminal justice system. Police officers may not freely select any means for obtaining information from suspects during post-arrest interrogations; their policies and practices for questioning people in custody are shaped by rules enunciated in Supreme Court decisions. Prosecutors are not free to employ their own selection criteria in seeking to choose jurors who will convict defendants; they must adhere to Supreme Court decisions forbidding racial discrimination in the selection of jurors. Corrections officials cannot arbitrarily punish prisoners through any means that they may choose; they must adhere to the Supreme Court's requirements concerning due process and appropriate punishments.

Legal issues concerning criminal punishment pose special difficulties for the Supreme Court that extend beyond the basic responsibility for safeguarding the fundamental constitutional value of individual liberty. As noted by McCloskey, many of the Constitution's phrases are ambiguous and those affecting the government's power to punish criminal offenders are no exception. In particular, the right to "due process of law" contained in the Fifth and Fourteenth Amendments and the Eighth Amendment's prohibition on "cruel and unusual punishments" challenge the justices' ability to reach a socially palatable interpretive consensus that upholds constitutional values. Moreover, issues of criminal punishment are complicated by the fact that claimants are individuals who have earned or are believed to have earned their despised status in society through harmful and indeed, sometimes horrifying, actions that violate established rules of law. Natural sympathies, which the human beings beneath the black judicial robes may feel for innocent citizens whose rights are violated, are not likely to exist in cases concerning criminal punishment in which despised citizens are alleging rights violations. Indeed, Supreme Court justices may find it extremely difficult to set aside their natural antipathy for particular offenders. Because Supreme Court justices' decisions are shaped by their personal attitudes and values as citizens who reside within a society racked by violence and crime (Segal and Spaeth 1993), issues concerning criminal punishment may be especially difficult to decide in accordance with the ideals of fundamental constitutional values.

This book will examine the Supreme Court's decisions affecting criminal punishment in light of changes in the high court's composition. During the 1970s, 1980s, and early 1990s, the Supreme Court's composition changed as Republican presidents appointed new justices who brought to the Court attitudes and values significantly different than those of their predecessors who decided cases in the 1950s and 1960s. The justices who served during the Warren Court era (1953-1969) drastically altered the meaning and policy implications of the Constitution by providing broad protections for rights and liberties, including those of criminal defendants and convicted offenders. According to Thomas Walker and Lee Epstein (1993, 19), Chief Justice Earl Warren "presided over what can only be described as a constitutional revolution, generated by a group of justices who were perhaps the most liberal in American history."

As the Warren Court justices retired during the 1970s, 1980s, and early 1990s, Republican presidents occupied the White House and used their appointment powers to nominate justices who were less supportive of broad rights for individuals. As indicated in Table 1, the Court's composition changed dramatically within twenty-five years. In 1968, the Warren Court was comprised of six liberal justices and three moderates with respect to voting records in non-unanimous criminal justice cases. By 1992, the Rehnquist Court was comprised of five conservatives, four moderates, and no liberals. While this drastic compositional shift on the high court affected legal doctrines for many

Table 1 - Ideological Composition Change on the U.S. Supreme Court, 1961-1993 (based on each justice's career percentage of support for individuals--"liberal votes"--in nonunanimous criminal procedure cases) [drawn from the Supreme Court Judicial Database]

YEAR	Liberal 67-100%	Moderate Liberal 50-66%	Moderate Conservative 33-49%	Conservative 0-32%
1961	4	0	5	0
	DGL-89		STW-45	
	BRN-76		FRF-44	
	WRN-74		WTK-41	
	BLK-70		HRL-38	
			CLK-33	
1968	6	0	3	0
	DGL-89		STW-45	
	FRT-83		HRL-38	
	MAR-80		WHT-33	
	BRN-76			
	WRN-74			
	BLK-70			
1984	2	1	2	4
	MAR-80	STV-64	BLM-42	OCN-28
	BRN-76		WHT-33	PWL-28
				BRG-19
				RNQ-15
1993	0	1	3	5
		STV-64	STR-44	KND-29
			BLM-42	OCN-28
			WHT-33	SCL-26
				TMS-20
				RNQ-15

Abbreviations: BLK-Black; BLM-Blackmun; BRN-Brennan; BRG-Burger; CLK-Clark; DGL-Douglas; FRT-Fortas; FRF-Frankfurter; HRL-Harlan; KND-Kennedy; MAR-Marshall; OCN-O'Connor; PWL-Powell; RNQ-Rehnquist; SCL-Scalia; STR-Souter; STV-Stevens; STW-Stewart; TMS-Thomas; WRN-Warren; WHT-White; WTK-Whittaker issues (Kairys 1993), the Rehnquist Court was less thoroughly conservative in its decision making than many observers believed (Smith and Hensley 1993). Indeed, the preservation of liberal doctrines concerning a right of choice in abortion (*Planned Parenthood v. Casey* 1992) and the prohibition on organized prayer in public schools (*Lee v. Weisman* 1992) demonstrated either that conservative justices adopted new, moderate positions on some controversial issues (Smith 1992) or that internal conflicts among the conservative justices prevented them from acting in unison to advance their policy preferences (Smith 1993c).

With respect to criminal justice issues, however, the conservative justices engaged in what John Decker (1992) has labeled a "Revolution to the Right." As this book will discuss, the changes in the Supreme Court's composition and decision making have had particularly dramatic effects on the criminal punishment issues of the death penalty, "cruel and unusual punishments" in prisons, and habeas corpus.

THE REHNQUIST COURT'S UNIQUENESS

The 1980s and early 1990s marked a notable period of change for the United States Supreme Court. Two conservative presidents, Ronald Reagan and George Bush, employed their constitutional power to appoint federal judicial officers as a means to replace retiring Supreme Court justices with new appointees who possessed judicial philosophies less supportive of broad rights for individuals. The Reagan and Bush appointees formed the nucleus of a new dominant majority within the Court that began to reshape the definition of constitutional rights and thereby alter the highest court's impact on a variety of public policy issues. Decisions by the new justices' predecessors defining the rights of criminal defendants and convicted offenders had been special targets of criticism by political conservatives. Subsequently, the reconstituted Supreme Court redefined constitutional provisions affecting criminal justice. As a result, the Court's impact on criminal justice institutions and policies changed.

What is the significance of the changes in Supreme Court decisions on criminal punishment and other aspects of criminal justice? Generally, the answer is determined by the eye of the beholder. To critics of the Warren Court's earlier decisions that provided constitutional protections for defendants and prisoners, the new Burger and Rehnquist era justices simply restored the federal judiciary to its proper, restrained role by deferring to the choices made by legislatures and law enforcement officials concerning appropriate criminal justice policies and practices. By contrast, to advocates of broadly defined constitutional rights, the Republican appointees improperly led the Court toward abdication of its responsibilities as the institutional guardian of the Bill of Rights and thereby created opportunities for criminal justice officials to engage in abusive practices. These general assessments emerge when observers view trends in Supreme Court decision making through the lens of particular political ideologies and policy preferences. A more complete evaluation of the Supreme Court's impact on criminal justice depends, however, not on perceived trends in judicial outcomes but on an examination of specific case decisions and their effects upon personal liberty and the administration of justice.

The "Warren Court" or any other chief justice's "Court" designates an era in which a chief justice served rather than a "court" that is statically composed of a particular set of justices. For example, the composition of the Supreme Court changed during Chief Justice Burger's lengthy tenure (1969-1986) through the appointments of Justices John Paul Stevens in 1975 and Sandra Day O'Connor in 1981. In addition, an individual justice changed his views on specific issues during that time period (i.e., Justice Harry Blackmun became more liberal). Thus, commentators spoke of there being more than one "Burger Court" (Kamisar 1983). In other words, these kinds of changes preclude the Supreme Court from making decisions in a consistent, classifiable manner during the tenure of a single chief justice. Why then is "the Rehnquist Court" worthy of examination?

It is appropriate to examine "the Rehnquist Court" because scholars' standard method for designating and analyzing Supreme Court eras is by marking the boundaries of those eras through the tenures of chief justices. Chief justices can be significant influences upon the Supreme Court if they use their positions to guide doctrinal developments through their authority to assign opinion authorship when they are in the majority or through their ability to organize majority coalitions (Danelski 1989). It is more useful to discuss the Supreme Court under Rehnquist as a "Court" than it would be for some other eras because the Court under Rehnquist is distinctive for its conservative composition. Its distinctiveness became further enhanced through personnel changes that added more conservative justices as aging liberals retired. Thus Chief Justice William Rehnquist, as a leading member of the conservative majority that determined the outcomes for most cases, could exercise his influence over the Court's opinions through his assignment power over authorship of opinions on behalf of the Court. By contrast, on the divided Burger Court, liberal Warren

Court holdovers such as William O. Douglas and William Brennan frequently made opinion assignments as the senior members of liberal majorities when Burger was among the dissenters.

In addition, the Rehnquist Court deserves its own examination because it marks the era in which conservative appointees took firm control of the Supreme Court in the form of a consistent, stable majority in most cases. The appointment of Justice Anthony Kennedy by President Reagan in 1988 altered the Court's previous tug-of-war between liberals and conservatives by tipping the Court's composition in a conservative direction. Because the conservative justices showed little reluctance to actively alter precedents with which they disagreed (Smith 1990c), the new conservative majority quickly made dramatic changes in Supreme Court precedents affecting issues such as employment discrimination (*Wards Cove Packing Co. v. Atonio* 1989). The conservative majority became stronger and more stable with subsequent appointments by President Bush in 1990 (David Souter) and 1991 (Clarence Thomas) to replace the Court's most liberal justices, William Brennan and Thurgood Marshall. The impact of Rehnquist-era conservative appointees is likely to be particularly pronounced on criminal justice because many of them are young enough to serve on the Court for decades to come (e.g., Justices Scalia, Kennedy, and Souter were in their fifties in 1995 and Justice Thomas was only in his late forties).

The Rehnquist Court differs from the Burger Court by the prominence of conservatives who have distinguished themselves as independent thinkers (i.e., Justice O'Connor), forceful and persuasive advocates of new approaches to decision making (i.e., Justice Scalia), and consistent conservatives on nearly all issues involving assertions of right by individuals (i.e., Chief Justice Rehnquist and Justice Thomas). Rehnquist was sometimes a lone dissenter during the Burger era because he was more conservative than the other conservative justices. With the altered composition of the Rehnquist Court, the new Chief Justice found himself among allies who shared his views about appropriate outcomes and thereby permitted him to influence doctrine through his majority opinion assignment powers. Indeed, G. Edward White (1988, 459) noted indications during the first years of the Rehnquist Court that the high court seemed notably different than the Supreme Court during the Burger era:

> [A] new majority might come into being that discarded the *ad hoc* centrism of the Burger Court....Continued personnel changes make the surfacing of such a majority...possible.... Regardless

of what style of decision-making or ideological inclination surfaces on the Rehnquist Court, it will be different from that of the Burger Court because the context of the Court's decisions, the personnel, and the issues the Court faces will all be different.

Because the Supreme Court is regarded as such an important influence over criminal justice practices in American society, the potent coalition of conservative justices on the Rehnquist Court had the opportunity to place an indelible stamp upon the criminal justice system that will remain for the foreseeable future. As the chapters that follow will illuminate, the justices' decision-making patterns, judicial philosophies, and evident policy preferences have profound effects upon judicial supervision of the criminal punishment and post-conviction legal processes. Decision making by the Rehnquist Court rapidly changed the federal judiciary's impact upon criminal punishment in a manner that was not merely an extension of the Burger Court's mixed decisions on criminal defendants' and prisoners' rights.

Moreover the impact of Supreme Court decisions on these issues affected larger numbers of people as the Court's composition changed. When the Warren Court had its most liberal composition from 1967 to 1969 (see Table 1), the national incarceration rate was less than 100 inmates per 100,000 population. By the time the Rehnquist Court reached its most conservative composition in 1993, the national incarceration rate was 351 inmates per 100,000 population (Cole 1995, 486). The most significant increases occurred during the 1980s and 1990s. In sharp contrast to the 329,000 people in prison in 1980, there were 1,053,000 people in prison in 1994 (Beck and Gilliard 1995, 1). These increases in the incarceration rate were produced through stiffer sentences mandated by state legislatures and massive prison construction programs. American sentences became so severe that even our close cousins across the border in Canada had occasion to refuse to extradite fugitive drug suspects because their judges regarded the length of prison sentences in the United States as "shocking" and contrary to basic human rights ("Canada Court" 1994). As a result, Rehnquist Court decisions affecting criminal punishment issues impacted tens of thousands of additional Americans and far more people than those affected by the decisions issued during earlier Court eras. Thus the changes in judicial doctrines initiated by the Rehnquist Court justices have assumed increasing importance in conjunction with punitive trends in sentencing and punishment practices.

CONTROVERSIAL PREDECESSORS: THE WARREN COURT

Chief Justice Earl Warren was appointed by President Dwight Eisenhower to a Supreme Court that included a few liberal justices, such as William O. Douglas and Hugo Black, who were eager to apply the provisions of the Bill of Rights against the states through the Fourteenth Amendment in order to expand the constitutional protections enjoyed by Americans. During Warren's tenure as chief justice (1953-1969), and particularly during the 1960s, the Supreme Court broadened the protections for criminal defendants and imposed upon state criminal justice officials the same rules that applied to federal officials. The pace of identifying rights contained in the Fourteenth Amendment's Due Process Clause quickened after the appointment of Warren-era justices (e.g., William Brennan (1956), Arthur Goldberg (1962), Abe Fortas (1965), and Thurgood Marshall (1967)) who were more receptive than previous justices to arguments concerning the expansion of constitutional protections for criminal defendants.

The Warren Court era produced many landmark criminal justice decisions that became the focus of criticism by politicians, the general public, and later Supreme Court justices. In *Mapp v. Ohio* (1961), a case concerning a warrantless search of a woman's home by Cleveland police officers, the Supreme Court applied the "exclusionary rule" to state and local law enforcement officials throughout the country. State and local officials came under the rule that had governed federal law enforcement since 1914: illegally obtained evidence could not be used in prosecuting criminal suspects. In the case of *Gideon v. Wainwright* (1963), the Supreme Court established that state courts had to provide legal representation for indigent criminal defendants facing six months or more of incarceration . This decision imposed upon the states the same Sixth Amendment obligations for provision of criminal defense counsel that had applied to the federal government since 1938. In the controversial case of *Miranda v. Arizona* (1966), the Court required police officers to inform arrestees of their right to counsel and their right to remain silent. The Warren-era justices incorporated the Sixth Amendment's right to trial by jury into the Due Process Clause of the Fourteenth Amendment for application to state courts in the case of *Duncan v. Louisiana* (1968). In *Johnson v. Avery* (1969), the justices declared that prisoners' right of access to the courts required correctional administrators to permit inmates to assist each other with legal petitions unless the state provided an alternative means of legal assistance for prisoners.

Many states had already imposed some of these rules (e.g., counsel for indigent defendants) upon themselves through legislative or judicial action, but the justices apparently felt that the nation needed uniform standards. According to Archibald Cox (1968, 87), "It would have been better if the States had reformed their criminal procedure..., but the simple fact is that a minority of States failed to act despite a long period of warning....[I]f one arm of government cannot or will not solve an insistent problem [e.g., coerced confessions, unlawful searches, unrepresented defendants, etc.], the pressure falls upon another. This has been a major factor in the Supreme Court's activity in the field of criminal law."

The foregoing cases as well as other Warren-era decisions placed the Supreme Court at the center of controversy and led many people to believe that the Court's decisions were diminishing the effectiveness of law enforcement and favoring the rights of criminals over the rights of law-abiding citizens. Even though state legislatures and state courts had implemented similar reforms in some states, the Supreme Court became the symbolic and practical target of criticism for implementing criminal justice guidelines throughout the country. In Christopher Wolfe's (1986, 271) view:

> [The Warren Court's imposition of the exclusionary rule] protect[ed] not merely the rights of the guilty parties,...but also those of...innocent persons who had been unconstitutionally searched but never appeared in court. But the Court inevitably opened itself to very substantial criticism when it imposed a rule that redounded in very obvious ways to the benefit of criminals....[and that did not strike] a reasonable balance between [the] important objectives [of effective law enforcement and protection of fundamental rights].

The Warren-era decisions that limited the discretion of law enforcement officials by expanding constitutional rights for criminal defendants unleashed a steady torrent of criticism that continued into the 1990s. As described by one critic, "In no other area of American life has the impact of the rights industry been more disabling than on the interlocking institutions of the law enforcement system. A full account of the mischief worked on law enforcement [since the 1960s] would be a life's work" (Morgan 1984, 74). Lest the critics' words distort perceptions about the Warren Court's decisions, it is important to remember that there were also decisions that went against defendants' asserted rights: "[R]hetoric about the Warren Court's consistent pro-defendant ("pro-criminal") stand masked the fact that the Court was certainly *not* uniformly pro-defendant. The justices had, for example, provided legitimation of the use of informants and of stop-and-frisk....[and] had generally refused to apply its new rulings retroactively" (Wasby 1976, 200). Although the Warren-era criminal justice decisions provided mixed results for defendants, the Supreme Court established important, highly publicized rights for defendants that attracted strong political opposition.

Social developments during the 1960s and thereafter undoubtedly exacerbated the hostility directed at Warren Court era decisions affecting criminal justice. During the 1960s, crime rates escalated dramatically. For example, although murder rates had been higher during the 1940s, they declined during the 1950s to only 4.5 per one hundred thousand population in 1962. However, by 1966, the murder rate had increased to 5.6 and by 1972 it had increased to 9.4, the highest rate since 1936 (Wilson 1983, 15). With memories of the relatively tranquil 1950s in mind, Americans perceived an enormous increase in street crime. In the 1960s, many factors contributed to the increased crime rate, including the huge cohort of "baby boomers" who passed through their "crime prone years" as teenagers and young adults and thereby generated a demographically inevitable increase in crime. Other factors added to the fearful perceptions about the pervasiveness of violent crime, including televised coverage of urban riots and police attacks on civil rights protesters as racial minorities asserted their right to equality. These events concerned issues other than crime, but they contributed to the public's perception of increased social disorder within American society. Because these developments occurred at the same moment that the Supreme Court expanded rights for criminal defendants and limited the discretionary authority of law enforcement officials, critics claimed that the Court's decisions actually contributed to the increase in crime. Although social science research discredits the claimed linkages between the expansion of rights for criminal defendants and the increasing crime rates (Walker 1989), the convergence of growing public concerns about crime and judicial decisions protecting defendants gave conservative politicians, particularly Richard Nixon and his successors Ronald Reagan and George Bush, an ideal issue for attracting electoral support.

IMMEDIATE PREDECESSORS: THE BURGER COURT

Richard Nixon campaigned as the "law and order" candidate in the 1968 presidential election. In his nomination acceptance speech at the

Republican National Convention, Nixon blamed the judiciary for contributing to the problem of crime in American society (Epstein and Walker 1992, 335):

> [L]et us also recognize that some of our courts in their decisions have gone too far in weakening the peace forces as against the criminal forces in this country. Let those who have the responsibility to enforce our laws, and our judges who have the responsibility to interpret them, be dedicated to the great principles of civil rights. But let them also recognize that the first civil right of every American is to be free from domestic violence.

Upon assuming the presidency, Nixon immediately had the opportunity to alter the political composition of the court which so disturbed him with its criminal justice decisions by replacing retiring Chief Justice Earl Warren with Warren Burger. Nixon appointed Burger, who was a federal appellate judge at the time, specifically because Burger was "a jurist known to be hard-nosed on questions of law and order" (Abraham 1985, 297).

During his tenure as president, Nixon also had the opportunity to appoint three more justices. Nixon filled a total of four seats on the Supreme Court because Lyndon Johnson, in his final year as a lame duck president, miscalculated the extent of his political power and saw his appointees, Abe Fortas for elevation to Chief Justice and Homer Thornberry for Fortas's Associate Justice seat, blocked by Senate Republicans who sought to save the appointments for what they hoped would be a new Republican president (Smith 1989-90). As a consequence of the resulting investigation and political attacks on Johnson's nominees, Fortas resigned soon after Nixon took office in the wake of controversies about outside compensation he had received while serving as an Associate Justice. If not for Johnson's efforts to appoint his cronies and his overestimation of his political strength, a Democratic appointee would have taken the seat of Warren and Fortas would have remained on the Court. Instead, Nixon was handed the opportunity to reshape the Court's composition.

After his first two nominees for Fortas's seat were rejected by the Senate, in 1970 Nixon appointed Harry Blackmun, a respected federal appellate judge who was a long-time personal friend of Warren Burger. During his first years on the Court, Blackmun fulfilled Nixon's expectations for conservative decisions through "a tough pro-state posture in criminal-justice cases, in particular those involving the exclusionary rule" (Abraham 1985, 303). When Justices Hugo Black and John Harlan retired in 1971, Nixon appointed two more conservatives, Lewis Powell and William Rehnquist. In considering possible nominees for these final two seats, Nixon and his advisors rejected at least one other finalist because they did not believe the candidate was strongly opposed to the Warren-era decisions affecting criminal justice (ibid., 307). By employing his emphasis on reducing the scope of rights for criminal defendants in his selection of Supreme Court appointees, President Nixon was able to reshape the composition of the Court within a relatively brief period of time. Unfortunately for Nixon, however, his appointees were less eager than he would have hoped to alter the criminal justice precedents established by the Warren Court.

During the Burger Court era, the justices reduced the scope of rights established by the Warren Court but did not overturn the Warren era landmark decisions. In fact, the justices expanded some rights for criminal defendants and prisoners. As one observer commented after the first six years of Burger's tenure as chief justice (Wasby 1976, 200):

> One might well have expected the Supreme Court under Warren Burger to engage in substantial retrenchment from Warren Court policy, particularly because Burger's criticisms of the new rules were clear even before he arrived at the high court. Yet both the exclusionary rule of *Mapp* and the warning requirement of *Miranda*, although suffering some erosion, remain essentially intact. Right to counsel at trial was extended. Remedies for deprivation of speedy trial were firmly enforced.

Although Burger was a vociferous critic of the exclusionary rule from the very beginning of his tenure as chief justice (*Bivens v. Six Unknown Named Agents of the Federal Bureau of Narcotics* 1971), he never persuaded his colleagues to abolish the rule. The conservative justices weakened the rule by creating a variety of exceptions for the inclusion of evidence despite improper police practices: inevitable discovery of evidence (*Nix v. Williams* 1984), good faith belief by police officers who erroneously think that they have valid warrants for searches (*United States v. Leon* 1984), and public safety situations (*New York v. Quarles* 1984). Instead of regularly expanding individuals' rights as the Warren Court had done, the Burger era evidenced an emphasis upon balancing the costs and benefits for law enforcement of recognizing or diminishing defendants' rights. Despite the reduction of some rights, upon Burger's retirement in 1986, the *Mapp* decision and other important decisions stood as weakened but still authoritative precedents.

During the Burger era, the Supreme Court instituted more vigorous requirements for ensuring fairness in death penalty decisions (*Gregg v. Georgia* 1976) and expanded some rights for prisoners (*Bounds v. Smith* 1977). However, the Court also provided clear limitations on how far they were willing to extend prisoners' rights (*Rhodes v. Chapman* 1981). As Stephen Wasby (1976, 201) has noted, "there were areas where the Burger Court refused to extend new protections, for example, the right to counsel in some post-trial situations, where it was likely the Warren Court would have done so."

Because the Burger Court era initiated the conservatizing process of limiting the rights that had been established during the Warren Court era, one could conclude that the Rehnquist Court era merely represents an extension of trends that began in the 1970s. Yale Kamisar (1987, 168) notes that "[N]ew...justices will feel more comfortable [in reversing Warren era precedents], and it will be more respectable to do so, because the [Burger] Court has stripped [the Warren Court] doctrines of their constitutional bases in recent years." For example, although the Warren era majority declared that the exclusionary rule was compelled by the Constitution, conservative justices during the Burger era argued that it was merely a rule created by judges to advance a public policy against police misbehavior. Thus the Burger Court set the stage for an erosion of criminal defendants' rights by the more conservative Rehnquist Court.

THE REHNQUIST COURT ERA

The Rehnquist Court era began in 1986 when the United States Senate confirmed Associate Justice William Rehnquist for elevation to Chief Justice after the retirement of Warren Burger. The Rehnquist era, like other Supreme Court eras, is defined by the decisions and interactions of the individual justices serving on the Court while Rehnquist is Chief Justice. In its criminal justice decisions, the Rehnquist Court continued and expanded the Burger Court's erosion of broad rights for criminal defendants and clear rules for law enforcement officials. With respect to *Miranda* warnings, the Court announced that police officials no longer needed to inform suspects of rights exactly as the Court had described in *Miranda*. Instead, officers could change the warnings, even at the risk of confusing the suspects, as long as they got the basic message across. Thus officers were permitted to tell a defendant that they might not be able to secure a lawyer for him even though he was supposed to be entitled to one (*Duckworth v. Eagan* 1989).

In other cases, the Rehnquist Court expanded the permissible contexts for warrantless searches and thereby reduced the potential coverage of the exclusionary rule. For example, in *Illinois v. Rodriguez* (1990), the Court declared that a non-resident girlfriend could give permission for police to enter her boyfriend's apartment, over which she had no legal authority, as long as the police reasonably believed that she resided in the apartment and possessed authority over the premises. Such decisions reduce the incentives for police to collect information carefully before asserting a basis for entering a person's home.

Presidents Reagan and Bush selected conservative individuals for appointment or, in Rehnquist's case, elevation, because they hoped that those individuals would apply their conservatism to the issues brought before the third branch of government. Thus the individual justices who comprise the Rehnquist Court are responsible for altering the high court's influence over the criminal justice system.

Chief Justice William H. Rehnquist

William Rehnquist, born in 1924, came from a middle-class family. After military service in World War II, he earned degrees at Stanford University and Harvard University before graduating first in his class from Stanford Law School in 1951. He served as a law clerk for Supreme Court Justice Robert Jackson before entering private law practice in Phoenix, Arizona. He established his conservative credentials during the 1950s by writing articles in national magazines criticizing the Warren Court for favoring the rights of Communists and criminal defendants (Davis 1989). He was politically active in Phoenix on behalf of Barry Goldwater's 1964 presidential campaign and in working to oppose anti-discrimination laws and school desegregation. He was brought into the Nixon Administration as an Assistant Attorney General in the office that provided legal advice to the President. His work for the Nixon Administration provided an indication of his views concerning criminal justice (ibid., 6-7):

> As the president's lawyer's lawyer, [Rehnquist's] principal duty was to draft position papers on the legality of the administration's actions. The positions he took in favor of, for example, inherent executive authority to order wiretapping, preventive detention, and abolition of the exclusionary rule exemplified

Rehnquist's agreement with the Nixon administration's attitude toward crime. He also shared the administration's abhorrence of student unrest.... If he had not shared the views of the administration, he would not have been selected for a position in the Justice Department. Still, he endorsed the policies with enthusiasm and energy.

When Nixon made Rehnquist a surprise nominee to the Supreme Court in 1971, Rehnquist was attacked for his work against civil rights laws, for a memo he wrote as a law clerk for Justice Jackson opposing *Brown v. Board of Education* (1954), and for his opposition to the civil liberties decisions of the Warren Court. He attracted substantial opposition but was confirmed by a 68 to 26 vote in the Senate (Abraham 1985, 313). Rehnquist is recognized as the Burger era's foremost advocate of judicial restraint, a philosophy described by Henry Abraham (ibid., 318) as "permitting legislatures...wide discretion in forging public policy and public law, even if...representatives enact silly, stupid, asinine, unnecessary, even unfair and undemocratic legislation." Rehnquist does not always defer to the decisions of other governmental decision makers, especially when those policy makers enact affirmative action laws designed to assist women and members of racial minority groups (*City of Richmond v. J.A. Croson Co.* 1989; *Regents of the University of California v. Bakke* 1978). This deviation from his stated judicial philosophy in the service of politically conservative decisions may provide evidence of his willingness to permit his policy preferences to override his philosophy when faced with a liberal legislative decision with which he disagrees. This seems especially true in his participation in statutory interpretation decisions that suddenly altered long-standing precedents by narrowing legislatively mandated protections for victims of employment discrimination (*Wards Cove Packing Co. v. Atonio* 1989; *Patterson v. McLean Credit Union* 1989).

In addition, Rehnquist's espoused philosophy of deference to other branches of government does not mean that he subscribes to another tenet of judicial restraint, namely "interpretive fidelity" or adherence to case precedent in order to create stability in law and preserve the legal image of the judiciary (Canon 1983). As Sue Davis (1989, 10) concluded from her analysis of Rehnquist's discussion of case precedent during his first confirmation hearings before the Senate Judiciary Committee:

Rehnquist's statements regarding the role of precedent implied that, in his view, precedent of recent vintage, particularly if established by a divided Court, may be overturned if a substantial majority of the Court agrees that the interpretation of the Constitution upon which that precedent was based was incorrect. His statements suggested that he would not have trouble voting to overturn the decisions of the Warren Court, particularly in the area of the rights of the accused.

In his performance as an Associate Justice and later as Chief Justice, Rehnquist consistently opposed assertions of claimed rights by criminal defendants and supported efforts to reverse the landmark criminal justice decisions of the Warren Court era. Rehnquist has objected to the Warren Court's application of the provisions of the Bill of Rights to state criminal justice systems and "his opinions in cases involving the rights of those accused and convicted of crime are notable for their consistent support for law enforcement" (ibid., 44). In "fulfill[ing] Richard Nixon's dream of a justice who would strengthen the 'peace forces' against the 'criminal forces'" (ibid.), Rehnquist urged abolition of the exclusionary rule, deference to state legislatures' decisions about applying the death penalty and other punishments, including mandatory life sentences for multiple theft offenses totaling less than $250 (*Rummel v. Estelle* 1980), and general loosening of judicial guidelines placed upon criminal justice officials. Because Rehnquist distinguished himself during the Burger Court era as the most conservative justice on virtually all issues involving individuals' rights, his elevation to Chief Justice faced significant political opposition, and he was confirmed by the relatively close Senate vote of 65 to 33 (Baum 1992, 51).

The Retirees

Three of the initial members of the Rehnquist Court retired and made way for new appointees who were significantly more conservative. Two later retirees, Justices Byron White and Harry Blackmun, were replaced by moderately liberal justices, Ruth Bader Ginsburg and Stephen Breyer, appointed by Democratic President Bill Clinton.

Justice Lewis Powell was born in 1907 and educated at Washington and Lee University and Harvard Law School. He was appointed to the Supreme Court by President Nixon in 1971 at the relatively advanced age of 64 after a distinguished career that included stints as president of the American Bar Association, the American College of Trial

Lawyers, and the Virginia State Board of Education (*Supreme Court at Work* 1990, 205). Although Powell was a Democrat, Nixon appointed him because he was a politically conservative patrician from the South whose appointment was intended to bolster Nixon's electoral support among Southern voters. Powell's performance as an Associate Justice earned him an image as a moderate. However, a careful empirical study of his decisions demonstrated that throughout his tenure (1971-1987) he usually joined the Court's conservatives in deciding cases (Blasecki 1990). Powell's reputation stemmed from several well-known decisions in which he joined the liberals to, among other things, support the right of choice for abortion (*Akron v. Akron Center for Reproductive Health* 1983), assert the right of illegal alien children to attend public schools (*Plyler v. Doe* 1982), and, most notably, approve the use of race-conscious affirmative action programs (*Regents of the University of California v. Bakke* 1978). In regard to criminal justice cases, Powell "lived up to some of [Richard Nixon's] expectations, especially in his supportive stance on...the state's power to administer criminal justice, where he and [Burger, Rehnquist, and O'Connor], sometimes joined by White or Blackmun, have tended to favor a good measure of state jurisdictional authority" (Abraham 1985, 309).

Justice William Brennan, born in 1906, was the son of a municipal government official. After graduating from Harvard Law School, he practiced labor law in Newark, New Jersey before becoming a state judge and, eventually, a member of the New Jersey Supreme Court. He was appointed to the U.S. Supreme Court in 1956 by Republican President Dwight Eisenhower in an apparent effort to impress Irish Catholic Democrats during an election year. Although Eisenhower had presumed that Brennan would be a moderate justice, he was sorely disappointed by the liberal decisions of both Brennan and Earl Warren. He later reportedly said that his decisions to appoint them to the Supreme Court were the biggest mistakes of his presidency (ibid., 263). Brennan worked closely with Warren to engineer liberal majority coalitions for landmark decisions throughout the Warren Court era. As the Burger Court era's foremost advocate of constitutional interpretation according to flexible ideals that would expand and protect broad rights for individuals (Mason and Stephenson 1987, 607), he eventually became the symbolic and practical target for conservative critics who sought reversal of the Warren Court's judicial legacy. Although he became a frequent dissenter in seeking to protect Warren Court precedents as the Court's composition became more conservative during the Rehnquist era, Brennan, who was regarded as the Supreme Court's most effective internal politician (Greenhouse 1990), managed to pull together slim majorities to preserve, at least temporarily, such concepts as affirmative action (*Metro Broadcasting v. Federal Communication Commission* 1990) and school desegregation (*Missouri v. Jenkins* 1990). Prior to his retirement in 1990, Brennan was a consistent supporter of individuals' assertions of rights violations directed against criminal justice agencies and officials.

Justice Thurgood Marshall was born in 1908, the son of a school teacher and a steward at a private club. After graduating from Howard University's law school, he became a renowned litigator for the National Association for the Advancement of Colored People (NAACP) in civil rights cases throughout the nation. He successfully argued numerous cases before the Supreme Court, including the famous case of *Brown v. Board of Education* (1954). He later became a federal appellate judge and then Solicitor General of the United States. When he was appointed to the Supreme Court by President Johnson in 1967, he became the first and only African-American justice until his successor, Clarence Thomas, was appointed in 1991. Throughout his tenure on the Supreme Court, Marshall was an ardent supporter of broad protections for individuals' rights in disputes against the government. He consistently joined the other liberals in the final years of the Warren Court and then, with Brennan, continued to defend Warren-era precedents during the Burger and Rehnquist eras.

These retirees' greatest impact on the Rehnquist Court came through their retirements. Brennan and Marshall had been fighting a losing battle against the conservative justices' efforts to erode the Warren Court's landmark cases affecting criminal justice. Their retirements in 1990 and 1991 respectively removed the Court's most dedicated defenders of constitutional rights for criminal defendants and created the opportunity for President Bush to solidify the emerging conservative majority through the appointment of two more conservative justices to the Court (David Souter and Clarence Thomas). Although Souter developed a relatively moderate voting record, he was much more conservative than his predecessor Brennan. Thomas was consistently conservative and drastically different than his predecessor Marshall. Although Lewis Powell had been consistently conservative on criminal justice issues, his replacement, Anthony Kennedy, was even more conservative on criminal justices issues as well as on other issues, such as abortion and affirmative action.

Justice Byron White was born in 1917. He earned degrees at the University of Colorado, Oxford University, and Yale Law School. White was a law clerk to Supreme Court Chief Justice Fred Vinson before returning to Denver to practice law. He worked on John F.

Kennedy's presidential campaign and became a deputy attorney general in the Kennedy Administration. Kennedy appointed White to the Supreme Court in 1962 as the replacement for retiring Justice Charles Whittaker (*The Supreme Court at Work* 1990). As a member of the Warren and Burger Courts, White was considered a "moderate" because he joined either the liberals or conservatives, depending on the issue in question: "[H]e joined the liberal majority on civil rights and reapportionment cases but was a consistent [conservative] dissenter in criminal justice cases and took a more modest view of First Amendment rights and federal power than did the majority of justices [on the Warren Court]" (White 1988, 433). Quirks of fate determine which justices leave the Supreme Court at which moments in history. By chance, the conservative members of the Rehnquist Court benefitted from the fact that by the end of 1991 the lone remaining member of the Warren Court (i.e., White) happened to be one of the few justices who had dissented against liberal criminal justice decisions in such cases as *Miranda v. Arizona* (1966) and *Escobedo v. Illinois* (1964), which concerned defendants' right to counsel during questioning. White retired in 1993 and was replaced by Ruth Bader Ginsburg, a more liberal Democratic appointee.

President Nixon appointed Justice Harry Blackmun in 1970 as a safe choice for confirmation after two other nominees to replace Abe Fortas had been rejected by the Senate. Blackmun was born in 1908 and earned his law degree from Harvard Law School before entering private practice, working as legal counsel for the Mayo Clinic, and then serving as a federal appellate judge. Although Blackmun initially joined his lifelong friend from Minnesota, Warren Burger, to provide a consistent conservative vote on the Burger Court, he later became more liberal. Analysts cite Blackmun's authorship of the controversial abortion rights landmark, *Roe v. Wade* (1973), as the point at which he began to support expansive interpretations of constitutional rights for individuals. However, he remained somewhat conservative when it came to criminal justice cases: "[After *Roe*,] Blackmun's jurisprudence appeared to begin actively to change....[w]ith the possible exception of the criminal justice-sector, where he would still more often than not be found at Burger's side" (Abraham 1985, 304). After the retirements of Brennan and Marshall, Blackmun automatically became one of the Court's two most liberal justices. His support for criminal defendants' rights was actually moderate when compared with the decisions of Brennan, Marshall, and other Warren Court justices. The Supreme Court's compositional shift toward conservatism had simply made the Court's moderates (Blackmun and Stevens) appear relatively liberal because all of the other justices were strongly conservative on criminal justice issues. Blackmun retired in 1993 and was replaced by Stephen Breyer, a Democratic appointee who is not central to this book's discussions because he had not yet participated in many of the Court's decisions.

The New Appointees

Justice Antonin Scalia replaced retiring Chief Justice Warren Burger in 1986 and thereby became an Associate Justice at the same time that Rehnquist became Chief Justice. Scalia, the son of a college professor, was born in 1936. After graduating from Harvard Law School, he practiced law with a large law firm, served as an attorney in the Nixon and Ford Administrations, and was a law professor at the University of Virginia and the University of Chicago before being appointed as a federal appellate judge. He was nominated for the Supreme Court by President Reagan because of his well-established reputation as an intelligent, outspoken political conservative. On the Supreme Court, Scalia quickly established himself as both a strident, articulate conservative and an independent thinker. Because he shares the other conservatives' beliefs about limiting the role of the judiciary in overriding decisions by other branches of government, Scalia became a consistent member of the conservative majority that emerged during the Rehnquist era (Brisbin 1990). Unlike Chief Justice Rehnquist, Scalia is willing to part company with the other conservatives when he believes that the Constitution clearly demands support for an individual's asserted right. His action in joining liberal justices Brennan, Marshall, and Blackmun to endorse flag burning as protected symbolic speech was the most notable example of his occasional willingness to assert judicial power against the policy choices of legislative and executive officials (*Texas v. Johnson* 1989; *United States v. Eichman* 1990). Scalia became a particularly important and influential member of the Rehnquist Court. Because of his willingness to write many concurring and dissenting opinions in order to assert rather than merely to explain his views, Scalia endeavors to move the other justices toward his particular approaches to statutory and constitutional interpretation. In criminal justice cases, Scalia consistently joined the conservatives except for a few notable deviations in Confrontation Clause and other cases in which he saw clear protections for individuals in the words of the Constitution (*e.g., Coy v. Iowa* 1988).

President Reagan appointed Justice Anthony Kennedy in 1988 to take the seat vacated by Powell's retirement. Kennedy, born in 1936, graduated from Harvard Law School and then worked as a private attorney and lobbyist in California before spending twelve years as a federal appellate judge. After Reagan had been embarrassed by the Senate's rejection of his outspokenly conservative nominee, Robert Bork, and Douglas Ginsburg withdrew his nomination because of public revelations that he had smoked marijuana as a law professor, the President looked to Kennedy as a non-controversial, solid conservative who could readily win approval from the Senate. On the Rehnquist Court, Kennedy has been a consistent member of the conservative majority on criminal justice issues and in other cases. He has written opinions advocating judicial restraint (*Missouri v. Jenkins* 1990) and he has joined opinions criticizing liberal decisions on such issues as abortion rights and affirmative action.

Fifty-year-old David Souter was appointed by President Bush to replace Brennan in 1990. Souter had earned degrees at Harvard and Oxford before returning to his native New Hampshire to practice law, work as the state's attorney general, and serve as a justice on the New Hampshire Supreme Court. Souter had just begun to serve as a federal appellate judge when Bush nominated him for Brennan's Supreme Court seat. Souter was a virtual unknown who possessed solid educational and legal credentials but had never taken public positions on controversial issues through speeches, writing, or political activities. Bush's selection of Souter appeared to reflect a desire to have a solid conservative confirmed by the Senate without the political problems that had surrounded the prior unsuccessful nomination of Judge Bork by President Reagan. During his Senate confirmation hearings, Souter evaded senators' questions about his specific views while he impressed them with his knowledge of Supreme Court cases and placated potential liberal opponents by praising Justice Brennan and defending Warren Court decisions. For example, Souter asserted that the *Miranda* decision did not create any new rights but merely represented a pragmatic method developed by the Warren Court to protect the existing rights for defendants. Souter also asserted that law enforcement officials have successfully adjusted to the burdens imposed upon them by *Miranda* (Lewis 1990). Although Souter's testimony portrayed him as a moderate, and he may eventually oppose the other conservatives' efforts to erase Warren Court landmarks, his initial performance as a justice showed him to be a consistent member of the conservative majority (Smith and Johnson 1992). In fact, during Souter's first term, he provided the decisive fifth vote in seven separate five-to-four decisions against assertions of rights by criminal defendants and prisoners that undoubtedly would have been decided the other way if Justice Brennan had remained on the Court (ibid., 39). During subsequent terms, Souter joined more frequently with the Court's moderates, such as Justices John Paul Stevens and Ruth Bader Ginsburg.

At age forty-three, Justice Clarence Thomas was appointed to replace Marshall in 1991. Thomas survived rancorous hearings, including nationally televised testimony about sexual harassment he allegedly undertook against a female employee, to win confirmation by the narrowest of margins, 52 to 48. Thomas was a graduate of Yale Law School who had worked for the Missouri Attorney General, a private corporation, a United States senator, and two federal agencies before spending one year as a federal appellate judge. In order to avoid creating an all-white Supreme Court, President Bush appointed Thomas, who was one of the relatively few conservative African American lawyers known for his vociferous criticism of liberal positions on affirmative action, abortion, and other issues ("Supreme Mystery" 1991). Because Thomas emulated Souter in evading specific inquiries about his views during the Senate confirmation hearings (Marcus 1991), his views on criminal justice and other issues remained to be demonstrated during his initial terms on the Court. His public record of speeches and articles created expectations that he would reveal himself to be another strong supporter of the conservative majority's efforts to reduce judicial guidelines that limit the decision-making discretion of government officials.

These appointees whose entire Supreme Court careers have been as members of the Rehnquist Court have two significant impacts upon the high court. First, they are all more politically conservative than their predecessors and therefore have strengthened the distinctive conservatism of the Rehnquist Court. The conservatizing effect of these appointments was enhanced by the fact that two of the appointees (Souter and Thomas) replaced two of the most liberal justices in the Court's history who were the primary remaining members of the Warren Court (Brennan and Marshall). Second, the appointees were all relatively young. In 1995, the four conservative newcomers ranged in age from forty-seven to fifty-nine and therefore were positioned to maintain their distinctive influence upon the Supreme Court through the first decades of twenty-first century.

Ruth Bader Ginsburg was appointed in 1993 by President Bill Clinton upon the retirement of Justice White. Ginsburg was educated at Cornell, Harvard Law School, and Columbia Law School. While serving as a law professor at Rutgers and later at Columbia, Ginsburg established herself as the leading legal advocate for gender equality as she led the American Civil Liberties Union's efforts to litigate gender discrimination cases. On behalf of the ACLU during the 1970s, she argued many of the most important gender discrimination cases before the Supreme Court. After President Carter appointed her to a federal judgeship in 1979, she served for twelve years on the U.S. Court of Appeals for the District of Columbia Circuit (Baugh, Smith, Hensley, and Johnson 1994).

Ginsburg's appointment raised high expectations that she might be able to push the Rehnquist Court in a more liberal direction. Her expected initial impact on criminal punishment cases was uncertain because she scrupulously avoided stating a position on capital punishment during her confirmation hearings despite being pressed on the subject by Republican senators (ibid., 10). As it turned out, her initial term demonstrated her to be more liberal than her predecessor Justice White, but she was not a new liberal spokesperson for the Court. Her voting record painted her as a moderate positioned between the three moderate justices [Stevens, Souter, and Blackmun] and the five consistently conservative justices [Thomas, Scalia, Rehnquist, O'Connor, and Kennedy] (Smith, Baugh, Hensley, and Johnson 1994).

President Clinton appointed Stephen Breyer to the Supreme Court in 1994 as the replacement for the retiring Justice Harry Blackmun. Breyer was a former Harvard Law professor who specialized in antitrust law. He served for several years on the U.S. Court of Appeals for the First Circuit in Boston before he was appointed to the high court. Because he had proven himself to be a moderate jurist on the court of appeals, he was not expected to have a major impact on criminal justice issues. During his confirmation hearings, he acknowledged that he recognized the constitutionality of capital punishment. An analysis of his first term performance placed him near the ideological center of the Supreme Court (Smith, Baugh, and Hensley 1995).

Continuing Holdovers from the Burger Court

Justice John Paul Stevens was born in 1920 and educated at Northwestern University's Law School. After law school, he became a law clerk for Supreme Court Justice Wiley Rutledge, practiced law with private law firms in Chicago, and served as a federal appellate judge. Because Stevens was a respected moderate who was not identified with any partisan ideology, his appointment to the Supreme Court in 1975 helped President Gerald Ford avoid accusations of partisanship in filling the seat of Warren Court liberal William O. Douglas, a justice who had been the target of impeachment initiatives by Ford when Ford was a member of Congress. On the Burger Court, Stevens established a reputation as an independent thinker who became more closely associated with the liberals' support for individual rights than with the conservatives' deference to government decisions (Abraham 1985, 325). Like Justice Scalia, Stevens frequently writes dissenting and concurring opinions, although his explanations for his opinions differ from Scalia's strident efforts to persuade the Court and otherwise lay the groundwork for changing future decisions. Although more moderate on criminal justice cases than Brennan and Marshall, Stevens, like Blackmun, became one of the Rehnquist Court's *de facto* liberals when his two liberal Warren-era colleagues retired.

President Reagan made good on his campaign promise to appoint a woman to the Supreme Court by nominating Sandra Day O'Connor in 1981 to replace Potter Stewart. Born in 1930, O'Connor had been a classmate of Rehnquist's at Stanford Law School. After the pervasive gender discrimination of the 1950s precluded her from working for major law firms, O'Connor worked in the public sector in Arizona and spent time away from lawyering raising her children. She became active in Republican party politics and served in the Arizona state senate and on the Arizona Court of Appeals before her appointment to the U.S. Supreme Court. Although she evinces sensitivity to issues of gender discrimination and has joined the liberals in decisions on some other issues, she has generally been a solid member of the conservative majority. Even when she disagrees with the conservatives, her disagreement may manifest itself in a concurring opinion expressing alternative reasoning rather than in opposition to the conservatives' preferred outcome in the case (*New York v. Quarles* 1984; *Employment Division of Oregon v. Smith* 1990). As the Court's only former state legislator, O'Connor places special emphasis upon reducing judicial supervision of state legislatures and state courts. Thus, on criminal justice cases, most of which challenge state laws or state judicial proceedings, O'Connor has been a consistent conservative: "[O'Connor] indicated a resolute tendency, albeit not...an ironclad one,...to back state court jurisdiction in the realm of criminal justice adjudication; to respect the finality of state court judgments; and to insist on the exhaustion of all remedies at the state level antecedent to permitting collateral review [of convicted offenders' cases] at the federal level" (Abraham 1985, 338).

Although the holdover justices included, after the retirements of Brennan and Marshall, the most liberal justice remaining on the Rehnquist Court (Stevens), he was much less supportive of individuals' rights in criminal justice cases than were his liberal Warren-era predecessors. Other Burger Court veterans, White and O'Connor, were supportive of individual rights for some kinds of cases but were consistently conservative in their approach to criminal justice cases. Thus they contributed to the distinctively strong conservative majority on the Rehnquist Court.

DETERMINANTS OF JUDICIAL DECISIONS

If justices' decisions were dictated by "law," there would be little interest in studying the factors that influence judicial decision making. In making decisions, justices would simply apply the governing precedents or the accepted constitutional theory. It is obvious, however, that judicial decisions are determined by something other than fixed legal rules or shared understandings of guiding principles. The modern Supreme Court has been comprised of decision makers who share common training in law school and common socialization as lawyers, yet they have manifested great disagreements among themselves about the proper interpretation of the Constitution and congressional statutes. Their approaches to judicial decision making and, consequently, their disagreements with each other stem from the justices' divergent philosophies, values, attitudes, experiences, and policy preferences that, until conservative justices gained a strong majority on the Rehnquist Court, caused the high court to split over many issues during the Burger era.

The vague wording of the Constitution, such as the phrase "due process of law," provides opportunities for justices to interpret the nation's fundamental law in accordance with their own particular visions of the desired distribution of governing power and the ideal degree of legal protection for human beings' rights. In addition, as the decision makers on the highest court in the land, justices can alter or reverse case precedents without any higher judicial body to limit the majority's new jurisprudential initiatives. Because, as Chief Justice Rehnquist (1987, 291) admits, "[t]he law is at best an inexact science....[so] [t]here simply is no demonstrably 'right' answer to the question involved in many of [the Supreme Court's] difficult cases," justices inevitably apply their values and policy preferences in attempting to produce the "best" result, as they see it, for American society. Thus presidents can, as Presidents Reagan and Bush demonstrated, influence the decisions of the Supreme Court by appointing justices who possess political values different from those possessed by the preceding justices whose decisions the presidents found objectionable.

Social science research on judicial decision making indicates that justices' (and other judges') decisions are determined by a variety of factors. As human beings, justices cannot separate themselves from the prevalent values of the historical era in which they live. Justices have sometimes made courageous decisions that clashed with dominant policies in society as, for example, when they attacked racial segregation in schools. More frequently, however, their decisions comport with the dominant political values of society. For example, a majority of justices demonstrated the fears that they shared with the general public about the country's fate in World War II by approving the summary incarceration of thousands of innocent Japanese-Americans (*Korematsu v. United States* 1944). Such a decision is extremely difficult to understand in light of the Constitution's requirement for "due process of law" before people are deprived of liberty, but it is easy to understand when the justices are recognized as human beings whose decisions are affected by social and political forces. As summarized in James Gibson's (1983, 32) careful review of the scholarly literature on judicial decision making, judicial officers' "decisions are [1] a function of what they prefer to do, [2] tempered by what they think they ought to do, but [3] constrained by what they perceive is feasible to do."

"What They Prefer To Do"

Supreme Court justices' decisions are guided largely by their personal policy preferences. As Lawrence Baum (1992, 145) observes:

> Choices among legally acceptable policies must be based on...factors [other than law]....[J]ustices come to the Court with strong views about many of the policy questions that they will be called upon to decide, and they develop strong views on other issues as they confront cases raising those issues. As a result, their policy preferences serve as a powerful force shaping how they view cases and choose among alternative policies. Like other policy makers, members of the Supreme Court make decisions largely in terms of their personal attitudes about policy.

The attitudes that underlie justices' policy preferences may stem from such sources as values learned from parents and teachers or perspectives gained from personal experiences. For example, research indicates that justices with prior professional experience as prosecutors tend to be less supportive of claims asserted by criminal defendants (Tate 1981). On the Rehnquist Court, many of the conservatives previously worked for government departments with prosecutorial responsibilities at either the county, state, or federal level. Although they may not have had direct responsibility for criminal cases themselves, the future justices worked as lawyers for the offices that planned and defended the decisions of government agencies and officials. O'Connor worked in a county attorney's office. Souter and Thomas worked in state attorney general offices, and Rehnquist, White, and Scalia worked for the U.S. Department of Justice. Such experiences potentially either reflect a disposition toward defending the government in conflicts with individuals, including criminal defendants, or serve as the basis for gaining such policy preferences through direct professional experience as advocates for governmental positions in cases concerning the enforcement of authoritative societal rules.

The same attitudes and values that cause people to affiliate with particular political parties subsequently lead judges from different political parties to assert differing policy preferences when determining judicial outcomes. Thus, not surprisingly, Republican justices tend to decide civil liberties and economic cases differently than Democratic justices (Tate and Handberg 1991). When Presidents Nixon, Reagan, and Bush sought to use their appointment power to alter Warren-era precedents supporting criminal defendants' rights, it is no surprise that they selected fellow Republicans (with the exception of Nixon appointee Lewis Powell) whom they perceived to share their policy preferences.

Several interrelated themes dominate the preferences and, consequently, the decisions of the conservatives who have altered the Supreme Court's role with respect to criminal justice. The Reagan and Bush appointees, including Reagan-elevated Chief Justice Rehnquist, emphasize arguments about judicial restraint that focus on a reduction in federal judicial influence over public policy and greater judicial deference to the legislative and executive branches of federal and state governments. The argument for judicial restraint relies on democratic theory to assert that policy decisions should be made by accountable government officials in the legislative and executive branches rather than by appointed judges who cannot be held accountable by the electorate. This philosophical approach creates risks that without the guardianship of the judiciary, political minorities (e.g., religious minorities, ethnic groups, poor people, criminal defendants, etc.) that lack the electoral power or wealth to influence legislatures will have their constitutional rights trampled by majoritarian political interests. Although the conservatives espouse this restraintist philosophy, this is not to say that the conservative justices always defer to decisions by other governmental entities. They have all participated in decisions asserting judicial power over policy choices by elected officials, especially when negating the liberal legislative policy of affirmative action (*City of Richmond v. J.A. Croson Co.* 1989). However, in the criminal justice context, it is easy for political conservatives to advocate deference to governmental decisions because such deference will produce outcomes supportive of traditional conservative preferences for unleashing law enforcement officials to pursue suspected street criminals vigorously and punish offenders harshly.

A related theme of making the federal courts less accessible to criminal defendants and prisoners serves the twofold purpose of reducing the federal courts' involvement in state criminal justice cases and alleviating the caseload burdens of the federal courts. For example, as chapter 4 will discuss in greater detail, Chief Justice Rehnquist and his conservative colleagues have worked consistently to narrow precedents and statutes that permit convicted offenders to challenge their convictions through collateral actions in federal courts after they have lost their appeals in state courts. The justices have also sought to limit the ability of prisoners to file civil rights lawsuits against state government officials for asserted violations of constitutional rights (Davis 1989). Rehnquist and his conservative colleagues have sought to limit access to the federal courts by claiming that state appellate courts' reviews of convictions are adequate and ought to be respected by the federal courts. Critics question the adequacy of state reviews because most state judges, as elected officials, lack the structural insulation from political pressures that enables federal judges to make unpopular decisions on behalf of a particularly despised minority, namely convicted criminal offenders. Another technique used by the justices to limit access to the federal courts is to decline to make retroactive Supreme Court decisions identifying rights violations by criminal justice officials. By limiting access to the federal courts, Rehnquist and his colleagues limit the opportunities for federal judges to interfere with the policies and practices of state criminal justice agencies and officials.

Justice Scalia has been particularly outspoken, although not unique, in his efforts to reduce the caseload pressures experienced by the federal courts. According to Scalia, the federal courts should be reserved for "the big case[s]" and therefore procedural and structural reforms should be imposed to limit the number of cases presented to the federal judiciary (Smith 1990a, 794). Chief Justice Rehnquist, as the administrative leader of the federal court system, has also repeatedly expressed serious concerns about the excessive burden placed on the federal judiciary (Rehnquist 1992). Such concerns have contributed to the Rehnquist Court's efforts to reduce claimants' access to the federal courts and to defer to decisions by state courts and governmental agencies.

An additional theme for the conservatives is an emphasis on federal judicial restraint not merely to enhance their preference for policy making by accountable elected officials but also to uphold the principles of federalism. Chief Justice Rehnquist and Justices O'Connor, Thomas, and Scalia, in particular, believe that the states should enjoy autonomy in making decisions about how they will administer their criminal justice agencies and other aspects of government without unnecessary interference by federal courts (*e.g., Garcia v. San Antonio Metropolitan Transit Authority* 1985). Their support for the principles of federalism extends beyond their desire to limit the power of federal courts. In a dramatic 1995 decision, a narrow five-member majority undertook, in the words of one observer, "a fundamental break with the way the court has interpreted the delicate balance between state and federal authority for the [preceding] 60 years" by limiting congressional power to legislate under the Commerce Clause (Fedarko 1995, 85). The Court invalidated the federal Gun-Free School Zones Act of 1990, which made it a crime to possess a firearm within 1,000 feet of a school, as an excessive exercise of federal legislative power (*United States v. Lopez* 1995). This decision has the potential to limit significantly the federal government's authority over criminal justice issues.

With respect to the relationship between state and federal courts, Rehnquist has specifically criticized the Warren Court's actions in nationalizing the Bill of Rights by interpreting the Fourteenth Amendment to require that the states adhere to the same specific requirements as the federal government. As Sue Davis (1989, 45) concluded from her exhaustive examination of the Chief Justice's performance during his first fourteen years on the Supreme Court, "[Rehnquist] has taken numerous opportunities to articulate his objections to the application of the provisions of the Bill of Rights to the states when the rights of the accused are involved." Like the other elements of their restraintist deference to state courts and legislatures, the Court's federalism theme implies an emphasis on finality of decisions and administrative efficiency rather than on careful certainty that proceedings are error-free and thereby advance the goal of equal justice under law.

The conservative justices' decisions that usually disfavor assertions of rights by criminal defendants and prisoners are consistent with and presumably a consequence of the policy preferences embodied within their version of a judicial restraint philosophy of judging. Not surprisingly, because most of the conservative justices gained their judicial appointments after active involvement with Republican party politics, such judicial outcomes are also consonant with contemporary Republican party positions. The shared aspects of the conservative justices' values and judicial philosophies produce common policy preferences and preferred outcomes in criminal justice cases. As a result, the new conservative majority has altered judicial involvement in criminal justice policy during the Rehnquist era.

Generational Impacts on Justices' Criminal Justice Decisions

In order to analyze the sources of justices' values, judicial philosophies, and policy preferences, one would have to examine justices' childhood socialization, parental influences, religious beliefs, and the entire range of influences over the development of individuals' attitudes and values. Although judicial biographers endeavor to undertake such analyses (*e.g.*, Hirsch 1981), it is extremely difficult to undertake a comprehensive historical analysis of sitting justices, especially because sitting justices are unlikely to cooperate with such research projects. For contemporary justices, scholars must look for clues that shed light on the influences that shaped or changed a specific justice's values or philosophy. For example, although Blackmun claimed that he moved from being a consistent conservative to a moderate liberal in order to provide more balance on an increasingly conservative Court (Wasby 1988, 251), scholars have linked his transformation to the extreme criticism he received from conservatives, including death threats, after his authorship of the abortion rights landmark, *Roe v. Wade* (Abraham 1985, 304). Alternatively, Scalia's judicial philosophy and values have been analyzed in light of his religious training and beliefs (Kannar 1990). With respect to the members of the Rehnquist Court's conservative majority, despite the lack of comprehensive evidence about the sources of each individual's values, their attitudes and policy preferences towards criminal justice can be linked to developments in American society that differed from those that affected the socialization of the Warren Court justices' generation.

Historically, American police officers were untrained patronage appointees of mayors and other local politicians who "enforced the narrow prejudices of their constituencies, harassing 'undesirables' or discouraging any kind of 'unwelcome' behavior" (Walker 1984, 84). Without judicial guidelines for their behavior or professional supervisors to establish and maintain standards, the police were relatively free to employ coercive and even violent methods against criminal suspects, especially when those suspects were poor, members of minority groups, or otherwise lacked status and political power in the community. The twentieth century movement to professionalize the police stemmed, in part, from scandals involving abusive police practices, such as the famous Wickersham Commission report in 1931 detailing brutal methods employed by many law enforcement agencies. The publicized scandals and criticisms of police practices in the 1930s contributed to efforts to reform police through civil service selection methods, education requirements, and professional training (Walker 1977).

Most of the justices on the Warren Court were born near the turn of the century and began their careers as lawyers by the 1930s. For example, only one (Potter Stewart) of the six justices who applied the exclusionary rule to the states in *Mapp v. Ohio* (1961) was not yet a lawyer by the early 1930s. All five justices (Warren, Douglas, Black, Brennan, and Fortas) who constituted the majority in the landmark *Miranda v. Arizona* (1966) decision requiring police to read suspects their rights were lawyers in the early 1930s. These justices were socialized into the legal profession at the moment in history when highly publicized abusive practices by unprofessional law enforcement officers placed reform on the national agenda and initiated the process of professionalizing American police departments through stricter hiring criteria, training, and civil service tenure protection. Moreover, several of the justices had actual personal knowledge of abusive law enforcement practices prior to the post-1930s police reforms. Chief Justice Warren had observed and even participated in coercive interrogations during his tenure as a California prosecutor in the 1930s (White 1982). Thus it was no surprise that he devoted much of his *Miranda* opinion to describing documented abuses by police seeking to obtain confessions from suspects. Justice Douglas's (1974, 78) autobiography describes his skepticism of police based on his observations of their behavior as a poor youth in Yakima, Washington: "[The police] caused a close sifting of loyalties in a young man who felt the roughness of their hand. I knew their victims too intimately to align myself with the police." Similarly, Justice Black had opportunities to observe firsthand police practices in Alabama when he was a practicing attorney and police court judge prior to 1912. Justice Brennan saw his father, a labor union organizer, beaten and bloodied by the police (Eisler 1993, 19). While serving as a crusading civil rights lawyer, Thurgood Marshall was nearly lynched by a group of Tennessee law enforcement officers who had seized him on a dark country road (Rowan 1993, 111). Because they had personal knowledge of police misconduct and awareness of publicized scandals from early in the twentieth century, these Warren Court justices had strong reasons to manifest their skepticism about the risks of abusive law enforcement practices by creating clear rules for police behavior in the form of landmark decisions protecting defendants' rights.

Although police scandals provided the original impetus for the professionalization of police departments, the Warren Court decisions of the 1950s and early 1960s contributed to the professionalization process by giving law enforcement officials throughout the country clear guidelines for their behavior. In particular, the Warren Court informed police that improper investigatory practices in conducting searches or questioning suspects would result in the exclusion of the evidence obtained. Officers were also instructed to take specific steps to inform suspects about their right to remain silent and their right to counsel prior to questioning. As a result of the twin motivating forces of early scandals and later Warren Court decisions, by the early 1960s police officers were increasingly civil service employees with professional training rather than simply uneducated, political patronage appointees.

In contrast to the Warren Court justices, many of the members of the Rehnquist Court's conservative majority learned about the criminal justice system and became socialized into the legal profession *after* the professionalization of police had already begun. Rehnquist and O'Connor became lawyers during the 1950s and did not have adult memories of the Wickersham Commission and other 1930s scandals. Scalia, Kennedy, and Souter entered the legal profession in the 1960s as the Warren Court accelerated the pressures for professionalization through judicial guidelines for proper police behavior. Because these justices came from later generations of lawyers whose knowledge of law enforcement agencies was based on police departments that had already moved toward professionalization, they lacked the Warren-era justices' personal experiences and memories that generated concerns about the risk of abusive behavior by the police. The Rehnquist Court justices have personal memories of the tranquil 1950s and the seemingly explosive growth in crime rates during the 1960s. While this awareness might encourage the justices to loosen the restrictions on police, their generational experience was not counterbalanced by a sufficiently concrete fear of abusive police behavior to provide a basis for overcoming their conservative philosophical inclination to defer to state governments. Thus, the newer justices' faith in professionalized police may lead them to undo some of the very Warren Court guidelines that contributed to the reassuring professionalization of police and the reduction in abusive law enforcement practices (Smith 1990b).

Decision Making on Criminal Justice in the Rehnquist Era

Scholars frequently draw inferences about the justices' attitudes, values, and policy preferences through rough empirical measures that compare their decisional patterns for particular categories of cases. Assessments of justices' liberalism and conservatism frequently come from evaluations of justices' rates of support for individuals who assert that their civil rights and liberties have been violated. As demonstrated by Table 1, the Rehnquist Court is comprised primarily of justices who usually do not support claims asserted by criminal defendants and prisoners. What is most notable about the table is the extent to which, in the wake of Brennan's and Marshall's retirements, proponents of constitutional protections for criminal defendants and convicted offenders lack a receptive audience on the Supreme Court.

As indicated by the foregoing discussion, conservative presidents succeeded in their efforts to reshape the Supreme Court's decisions affecting criminal punishment and other aspects of criminal justice by appointing new justices who were more conservative than their Warren-Court- era predecessors. The individual conservatives on the Rehnquist Court are not in complete agreement in every criminal justice case. However, even when specific conservatives decide to join the more liberal justices in supporting an individual's asserted rights in a given case, there are often enough remaining conservatives to form a majority that will produce an outcome adverse to individual claimants. The chapters that follow will discuss in detail how the Rehnquist Court's orientation toward criminal justice cases affected criminal punishment and the administration of criminal justice.

CHAPTER 2

Implementing Punishment:
Excessive Sentences
and Prison Conditions

Scholars' characterizations of the Rehnquist Court's decisions affecting criminal justice convey the impression of dramatic doctrinal changes that threaten the very existence of constitutional rights. John Decker (1992) says that the conservative Supreme Court has produced a "Revolution to the Right." David Kairys (1993, 179) opines that "there is certainly little left of due process." And Stanley Friedelbaum (1994, 141) concludes that "the future of defendant rights appears to be bleak." There are strong arguments favoring the validity of these conclusions in light of the trends that have taken place in Supreme Court decision making concerning Fourth Amendment, Fifth Amendment, and Sixth Amendment rights since the end of the Warren Court era. In reordering the values applied to the high court's judicial decisions, the Republican presidents of the 1970s, 1980s, and 1990s succeeded in appointing justices who would favor crime control over due process in many circumstances. Ironically, however, these generalizations are less clearly applicable for decisions affecting the treatment of the nation's most despised political minority, convicted criminal offenders. Convicted offenders' rights have never embodied more than limited protections. The scope of these protections has shrunk during the Rehnquist era, but the Court has not foreclosed opportunities for prisoners to raise claims under the Eighth Amendment.

Unlike presumptively innocent criminal defendants who theoretically share the same protections against unreasonable search and seizure (and other rights) as all citizens, convicted offenders have earned their despised status and seek protection in rights that have little relevance to the daily lives of the average law-abiding citizen. Under Eighth Amendment jurisprudence, this despised minority receives protection against disproportionate punishments that implicate the Cruel and Unusual Punishments Clause. In addition, they receive protection under the same constitutional provision against unconstitutionally harsh conditions of confinement in prisons. Pretrial detainees in jail are protected against excessive harshness by the Due Process Clause because they are not technically being subjected to "punishments" prior to conviction and therefore cannot be receiving cruel and unusual punishments (*Bell v. Wolfish* 1979). Despite the applicability of a different constitutional provision to unconvicted jail inmates, their Due Process protections are effectively guided by the standards established in the Court's interpretation of the Eighth Amendment's Cruel and Unusual Punishments Clause.

The Rehnquist Court has issued several important decisions affecting Eighth Amendment rights. Although these decisions reflect the conservative outlook produced by the Court's composition, they have not uniformly constituted wholesale doctrinal changes in the same manner as decisions affecting other aspects of criminal justice. With respect to proportionality in punishment, while the Court has not established strong protections for convicted offenders, the majority has resisted calls from Justices Scalia and Thomas to take the drastic step of abandoning proportionality as a legitimate consideration. In examining conditions of confinement, the Court has relaxed judicial supervision of correctional institutions yet has supported prisoners' claims in several cases and rejected the Scalia-Thomas argument for withdrawal of constitutional protection for prison inmates.

The less aggressive posture manifested by the conservative justices in these cases appears to stem from two factors. First, most Supreme Court cases establishing protections for convicted offenders were produced by the relatively conservative Burger Court rather than by the infamously liberal Warren Court. Because most of these decisions are not directly associated with the Warren Court era, they have not been treated as iconic liberal symbols ripe for attack and reversal by conservative critics who have continuously trumpeted their displeasure about *Mapp v. Ohio* (1961), *Miranda v. Arizona* (1966), and other Warren Court decisions. Conservatives have been more preoccupied in condemning the actions of federal district judges who implemented constitutional doctrines by taking over the administration of poorly and inhumanely managed prisons (Popeo and Smith 1987). Second, the idea that the Eighth Amendment contains standards for prison conditions that must be implemented through judicial supervision seems to have become accepted as part of a general value consensus shared by most conservative justices. Unlike the "hands-off" doctrine that previously characterized judges' attitudes toward correctional administration for most of American history, the decisions of the Burger Court and revelations about horrific conditions in many prisons have generated a wide understanding of the need for minimum standards for prisons. Even Chief Justice Rehnquist, a frequent critic of judicial decisions protecting defendants' and prisoners' rights, has acknowledged the need to maintain some judicial supervision of standards-enforcing rights. According to Rehnquist (*Bell v. Wolfish* 1979, 562),

> There was a time not too long ago when the federal judiciary took a completely "hands-off" approach to the problem of prison administration. In recent years, however, these courts largely have discarded this "hands-off" attitude and waded into this complex arena. The deplorable conditions and Draconian restrictions of some of our Nation's prisons are too well known to require recounting here, and the federal courts have rightly condemned these sordid aspects of our prison systems.

Thus the conservatism of the Rehnquist Court's decisions in non-capital Eighth Amendment cases has been less aggressively reactionary than in other areas of constitutional jurisprudence. As a result, an examination of these criminal punishment issues shows an element of the actual complexity of a Court that is often reflexively characterized as marching unwaveringly in lock-step conservatism. Consistent with empirical studies showing the Rehnquist Court has been less thoroughly conservative than many observers believe (Smith and Hensley 1993), these Eighth Amendment issues reveal a Court majority that has resisted extremists' efforts to withdraw constitutional protections from convicted offenders.

HISTORICAL BACKGROUND

For most of American history, the U.S. Supreme Court did not consider cases concerning criminal punishment. Because most state constitutions contained prohibitions on cruel and unusual punishment (Berkson 1975, 9) and the Supreme Court did not apply the Eighth Amendment to state governments until the 1960s (*Robinson v. California* 1962), most litigation challenging the legal validity of criminal punishments was focused in state courts (Wallace 1994). In the last quarter of the nineteenth century, the Supreme Court heard cases challenging methods of capital punishment, including public execution by firing squad (*Wilkerson v. Utah* 1879) and the newly-invented electric chair (*In re Kemmler* 1890), but the Court did not interfere with governmental choices about how to impose punishment.

The Court's first important case addressing the issue of the proportionality of non-capital sentence arose in the case of *O'Neil v. Vermont* in 1892. John O'Neil was convicted of unlawfully selling liquor in Vermont. He was found guilty of 307 counts and fined $20 for each count, plus court costs. He was required to pay $6,638.72 and, as part of his punishment, sentenced to imprisonment for three days for each dollar that he did not pay. Thus his imprisonment sentence equaled more than fifty-four years of incarceration (Berkson 1975, 65). Although the U.S. Supreme Court rejected his claim on procedural grounds and reaffirmed that the Eighth Amendment did not protect O'Neil or anyone else from punishment by a state, the case elicited the expression of dissenting views by three justices. Thus the *O'Neil* case provided the initial vehicle for U.S. Supreme Court justices, albeit a minority of them, to present publicly arguments favoring the application of Eighth Amendment principles to bar excessive punishments that are disproportionate to the crime committed.

The Supreme Court's initial landmark decision came in *Weems v. United States* in 1910. During the time that the Philippine Islands were under American jurisdiction, Paul Weems, a disbursing officer for the Philippine Branch of the U.S. Bureau of the Coast Guard and Transportation, was convicted for falsifying payroll records. He falsely recorded that he had paid out 204 pesos and 408 pesos to employees at two lighthouses. The statute provided for a minimum punishment of twelve years hard labor in chains, loss of citizenship rights, and a fine (Berkson 1975, 66). Weems actually received a sentence of fifteen years at hard labor. However, he successfully pursued his excessive punishment claim in the U.S. Supreme Court. The Court compared the sentence applied to Weems with lesser sentences mandated by statute for more serious violent offenses and found that his sentence violated the Eighth Amendment by being disproportionate to his offense. According to Justice McKenna's opinion, "There are degrees of homicide that are not punished so severely nor are the following crimes: misprision of treason, inciting rebellion, conspiracy to destroy the Government..., robbery, larceny, and other crimes" (*Weems v. United States* 1910, 380). In utilizing the Eighth Amendment for a proportionality claim, the Supreme Court broke new ground for the federal constitution, although state courts had already been developing such doctrines in interpreting the prohibitions on cruel and unusual punishments in their own state constitutions (Berkson 1975, 68).

Because the Court did not apply the Eighth Amendment to the states until the 1960s, the *Weems* decision affected few cases. During the 1950s, however, the Warren Court took a major step toward defining the meaning of proportionality under the Eighth Amendment. The *Weems* case and subsequent decisions gave little guidance about how to determine if a sentence was so disproportionate that it violated the Eighth Amendment. Judges were essentially left to react to stiff sentences to see if their consciences were shocked by the punishments. Appellate judges were usually reluctant to find Eighth Amendment violations because, as Larry Berkson notes, they were generally not eager to substitute their personal judgments for those of legislators and trial court judges (ibid., 71). In *Trop v. Dulles* in 1958, the Warren Court gave greater, albeit still murky, definition to the concept of cruel and unusual punishment and effectively reaffirmed the need for appellate judges to review questionable federal sentences.

Albert Trop was a twenty-year-old, native-born American citizen who served in the U.S. military in North Africa during World War II. While stationed in French Morocco in 1944, he was confined to a military stockade for violating disciplinary rules. Because he felt that conditions inside the stockade were intolerable, he escaped but changed his mind less than one day later and surrendered himself to the occupants of a passing Army vehicle. A general court-martial convicted Trop of desertion and he received a sentence of three years at hard labor, forfeiture of pay, and a dishonorable discharge. After Trop served his sentence and returned to civilian life, he applied for a passport in 1952 and learned that he and seven thousand other men had lost their citizenship under the Nationality Act of 1940, which mandated such forfeiture for soldiers convicted of wartime desertion.

In an opinion by Chief Justice Earl Warren, the Supreme Court determined that denationalization was unconstitutionally cruel and unusual because "[i]t is a form of punishment more primitive than torture, for it destroys for the individual the political existence that was centuries in development....His very existence is at the sufferance of the country in which he happens to find himself" (*Trop v. Dulles* 1958, 101). More importantly, Chief Justice Warren articulated a standard for interpreting and defining the Eighth Amendment. According to Warren, "the words of the Amendment are not precise, and...their scope is not static. The Amendment must draw its meaning from the evolving standards of decency that mark the progress of a maturing society" (ibid., 100). Although the words "evolving standards of decency" are vague, they indicate that judicial officers are supposed to judge Eighth Amendment cruel and unusual punishment claims by assessing how a punishment comports with contemporary societal standards. This guidance, as vague as it may be, provided a reference point for federal judges, including later justices of the Supreme Court, for determining the constitutionality of criminal punishments.

The application of the Eighth Amendment to the states came in *Robinson v. California* in 1962. Lawrence Robinson was convicted under a California statute that made it a crime to be addicted to narcotics. He was not caught buying, selling, possessing, or using illegal narcotics. His conviction was based on a police officer's testimony that the scars on Robinson's arm were consistent with scars normally exhibited by people who inject themselves with illegal narcotics. The Supreme Court declared that the statute violated the Eighth Amendment by criminalizing a *status* instead of a *criminal act*. The decision made actions by state and local officials susceptible to federal judicial scrutiny according to Eighth Amendment standards, but it did not explain how the Eighth Amendment was to be applied except with respect to the invalidation of status offenses. Justice Potter Stewart's opinion alluded to contemporary values when he declared that narcotics addiction is recognized as an illness and "in light of contemporary human knowledge, a law which made a criminal offense of...a disease would doubtless be universally thought to be an infliction of cruel and unusual punishment in violation of the Eighth [Amendment]" (*Robinson v. California* 1962, 666).

During the early 1960s as the Warren Court justices opened the door to judicial scrutiny of Eighth Amendment standards in state courts, they also created the opportunity for similar reviews of constitutional standards in correctional institutions. In 1961, the Court made the federal Civil Rights Statute (42 United States Code section 1983) a powerful vehicle for citizen litigation by permitting civil rights lawsuits in the federal courts when there are claims that state officials, including corrections officers, have violated individuals' constitutional rights (*Monroe v. Pape* 1961). In *Cooper v. Pate* in 1964, the Court declared that prisoners could use this federal statute to file lawsuits against corrections officials and facilities alleging violations of their constitutional rights. As the courthouse door opened to prisoner lawsuits, the African American adherents to the tenets of Islam played a leading role in asserting violations of constitutional rights, especially rights to freedom of religion that were frequently violated by corrections officials who were suspicious of these unfamiliar, militant prisoners (Smith 1993a). As the 1960s and 1970s proceeded, courts became more receptive to civil rights lawsuits by prisoners and gradually recognized the existence of a variety of rights possessed by prisoners concerning religious freedom, due process, and access to the courts (Call 1995).

While the Warren Court created the opportunity for judges to apply the Eighth Amendment to conditions in correctional institutions, the Supreme Court did not embark upon that course of action during Earl Warren's tenure as chief justice. The actual application of the Eighth Amendment to such institutions came during the Burger Court era. Relevant cases were decided first by lower court federal judges using the Warren Court's orientation toward protecting constitutional rights and later by the Burger Court itself (Berkson 1975). In 1970 a federal judge in Louisiana found that conditions in the Orleans Parish Prison were so horrible that they violated the Eighth Amendment's prohibition on cruel and unusual punishments (*Hamilton v. Schiro* 1970):

> [T]he jail was built in 1929 to house 400-450 prisoners, and...at the time, 800-900 prisoners were incarcerated there....The toilets were so badly rusted and corroded that cleanliness was impossible, and in some cells they had to be used as hand basins....The mattresses were never cleaned and were covered with vomit and urine....The roof and walls leaked. The jail was infested with rats, mice, and roaches....The threat of fire and of contamination by contagious diseases was great (Berkson 1975, 146).

Similar conditions were evident in various jails and prisons throughout the country. Beginning in 1970, here and there, judges began to declare that these facilities violated the Eighth Amendment and ordered that the deficient conditions be remedied. The problems in some prisons were compounded by the use of prisoner-trusties who were given free rein to terrorize, victimize, and even murder other prisoners as an inexpensive means to maintain order within the institutions. In 1970, a federal judge identified such problems in the Arkansas prison system and applied the Eighth Amendment's prohibition on cruel and unusual punishments to order drastic reforms (*Holt v. Sarver* 1970).

The Burger Court's initial non-capital Eighth Amendment decision was in the 1976 case of *Estelle v. Gamble*. J.W. Gamble's back was injured when a bale of cotton fell on him as he unloaded a truck while undertaking his prison work assignment. Although he continued to complain about severe pain and lingering medical problems, the prison doctor certified his capability to return to work after giving him painkillers and muscle relaxants for a month. Gamble refused to return to work because of his pain and he became subject to prison discipline, including administrative segregation for his refusal, even as the prison medical staff prescribed more medications for him. Gamble filed suit and his case arrived at the Supreme Court with the question of how the Eighth Amendment might apply to situations of prisoners' complaints about inadequate medical care. Although Gamble did not prevail in the Supreme Court, his case served as the vehicle for further clarification of the Eighth Amendment's definition and applicability to non-capital contexts.

Justice Thurgood Marshall's majority opinion used the *Trop v. Dulles* concept of contemporary standards in declaring that "[t]he infliction of unnecessary suffering is inconsistent with contemporary standards of decency" (*Estelle v. Gamble* 1976, 104). Marshall enunciated an Eighth Amendment-based rule with respect to prisoners' right to medical treatment: "We therefore conclude that deliberate indifference to serious medical needs of prisoners constitutes the 'unnecessary and wanton infliction of pain' ...proscribed by the Eighth Amendment" (ibid.). In using the phrases "infliction of unnecessary suffering" and "unnecessary and wanton infliction of pain," Marshall was drawing from the Burger Court's capital punishment cases to express the updated and more precise formulation of Chief Justice Warren's original effort to define an Eighth Amendment standard in *Trop v. Dulles*. These phrases were used in subsequent Burger Court cases as the standards for determining whether or not Eighth Amendment violations had occurred.

The lone dissenter in the case, Justice John Paul Stevens, complained that the Court had improperly created a subjective standard for determining Eighth Amendment violations that depended on the thoughts and motivations in the minds of corrections officials rather than an objective assessment of the treatment provided to prisoners. According to Stevens, "whether a constitutional standard has been violated should turn on the character of the punishment rather than the motivation of the individual who inflicted it" (ibid., 116).

The Court's opportunity to apply the Eighth Amendment to the larger issue of a prison's conditions of confinement came when litigation from Arkansas reached the high court. By the time of the Court's decision in *Hutto v. Finney* in 1978, the Arkansas prisons had been affected for eight years by decisions from lower federal judges. The justices were asked to decide whether these federal judges had exceeded their authority in establishing a minimum diet for prisoners, limiting periods of disciplinary confinement, and limiting the number of prisoners per cell. The facts underlying the Arkansas litigation epitomized the worst of conditions in correctional institutions with prisoner-trusties torturing other prisoners with a homemade electric-shock device, food served to prisoners falling below the minimum caloric level needed for healthy human survival, and groups of prisoners, including those with infectious diseases such as hepatitis, jammed into tiny cells together (*Hutto v. Finney* 1978, 682). In the majority opinion upholding the lower courts' remedial orders, Justice Stevens listed the tests to be applied to identify Eighth Amendment violations: "The Eighth Amendment's ban on inflicting cruel and unusual punishments....prohibits penalties that are grossly disproportionate to the offense,...as well as those that transgress today's 'broad and idealistic concepts of dignity, civilized standards, humanity, and decency'" (ibid., 685). The Stevens opinion focused on the objective Eighth Amendment formulations rather than the subjective standard applied to medical treatment in *Estelle v. Gamble*. Justice Rehnquist dissented and questioned whether the prison's practices had been shown to violate the Constitution (ibid., 710).

While the *Hutto* case signaled to federal judges around the country to continue their enforcement of Eighth Amendment standards in correctional institutions throughout the country, commentators regard the case as marking the end of the Prisoners' Rights Era before the Supreme Court entered a new era of deference to correctional authorities (Call 1995). The 1979 case of *Bell v. Wolfish* is regarded as heralding a halt to the expansion of judicial activity to identify and protect prisoners' rights. The case included a number of assertions of rights violations including a claim that double-bunking in rooms designed for individual occupancy at the federal Metropolitan Correctional Center (MCC) in New York City violated the Eighth Amendment's prohibition on cruel and unusual punishments. The Court of Appeals rejected the Eighth Amendment claim because the pretrial detainees in the MCC were not yet being "punished" and therefore their confinement did not constitute punishment as covered by the Eighth Amendment. When the case reached the Supreme Court, the justices considered and rejected the double-bunking claim by analyzing the detainees' right to not be deprived of liberty without due process of law under the Fifth Amendment. Although the decision was based on the Fifth Amendment, it was a precursor to an Eighth Amendment prison case that raised the issue as a violation of the prohibition on cruel and unusual punishments.

In *Rhodes v. Chapman* in 1981, the Court rejected a similar double-bunking claim in a state prison with cells designed to each hold a single prisoner. Justice Lewis Powell's majority opinion reaffirmed the Court's application of contemporary values to define the Eighth

Amendment, but warned lower court judges against acting too aggressively to reform prisons. According to Powell, "[C]onditions that cannot be said to be cruel and unusual under contemporary standards are not unconstitutional. To the extent that such conditions are restrictive and even harsh, they are part of the penalty that criminal offenders pay for their offenses against society" (*Rhodes v. Chapman* 1981, 347). Powell reinforced the application of objective standards for identifying Eighth Amendment violations by declaring that unconstitutional practices must violate "contemporary standard[s] of decency," involve "wanton and unnecessary infliction of pain," or result in "unquestioned and serious deprivations of basic human needs" (ibid.). The Burger Court majority's growing orientation toward deference to corrections officials was evident in Powell's statement that "courts cannot assume that state legislatures and prison officials are insensitive to the requirements of the Constitution or to the perplexing sociological problems of how best to achieve the goals of the penal function in the criminal justice system" (ibid., 352).

The Burger Court addressed the proportionality issue in a pair of cases in the early 1980s. In *Rummel v. Estelle* in 1980, a narrow majority of justices approved a life sentence imposed by Texas upon a "habitual offender" who was convicted of three offenses that involved stealing $80 in 1964, $28.36 in 1969, and $120.75 in 1973. The Court determined that a life sentence was not a disproportionate punishment for stealing $229.11 over a nine-year period. By contrast, a narrow majority of justices in *Solem v. Helm* in 1983 invalidated a life sentence imposed by South Dakota on a "habitual offender" convicted of multiple non-violent offenses, including burglary, drunk driving, and "uttering a no account check." The *Solem* decision did not overturn *Rummel* but rather distinguished the two cases because Texas permitted parole eligibility for life-sentenced habitual offenders while South Dakota precluded parole release for such offenders. In fact, individual justices were consistent in their belief that such life sentences are either permissible or impermissible, but Justice Harry Blackmun apparently found the parole eligibility distinction persuasive and therefore switched sides between the two cases. In essence, the two cases demonstrated that the Burger Court justices were deeply divided in their conceptions of the meaning of the Eighth Amendment's proportionality requirement.

In the final relevant decision of the Burger Court era, the justices returned to a subjective standard for cases involving allegations of excessive use of force by corrections officials. In *Whitley v. Albers* in 1986, a prisoner was shot by a corrections officer during an inmate uprising. The prisoner filed suit claiming that the officer's action constituted cruel and unusual punishment. In the case, the inmate alleged that he was shot despite not being part of the uprising and not making any threatening actions toward the officer. The Court decided that in the context of prison conflicts that justify actions by officials to restore security and order, a prisoner cannot succeed in claiming a rights violation unless the prisoner can show that prison officials acted "maliciously and sadistically for the very purpose of causing harm" (*Whitley v. Albers* 1986, 321). Thus, as in the medical treatment context, the Court established a standard involving an examination of prison officials' motivations and state of mind rather than looking objectively at the action taken and the harm inflicted.

As indicated in the foregoing review of Supreme Court decisions, it was the Burger Court rather than the Warren Court that was primarily responsible for tackling and establishing legal standards for non-capital Eighth Amendment cases concerning proportionality in punishment and prison conditions. Thus the precedents examined by the Rehnquist Court when it faced such issues were those established by a conservative-dominated Supreme Court, many of whose members continued to serve during the Rehnquist Court era. Unlike other issue areas concerning constitutional rights, the conservative justices on the Rehnquist Court era did not find themselves confronting and reacting against Warren Court precedents that had assumed the status of symbolic and substantive targets in the rhetoric of conservative politicians.

THE REHNQUIST COURT ERA

During the first few terms of the Rehnquist Court era, the justices' Eighth Amendment cases focused on capital punishment and related issues. At the close of the 1990-91 term, however, the Court issued two important decisions interpreting the Eighth Amendment in non-capital contexts: *Harmelin v. Michigan* (1991), concerning the Eighth Amendment's proportionality requirement, and *Wilson v. Seiter* (1991), concerning constitutionally sufficient prison conditions. The Court's decisions in these cases were determined by the appointment of Justice David Souter to replace retiring Justice William Brennan. Because Souter's first-term voting pattern indicated that he was much less supportive of individuals' rights than Brennan had been (Johnson and Smith 1992), it appears that these two Eighth Amendment cases were among a dozen close decisions in which the arrival of Souter tipped the Supreme Court decisively in a new direction (Smith and Johnson 1992). In both Eighth Amendment cases, Justice Scalia led the Court in clear efforts to reshape Eighth Amendment jurisprudence in a manner that would narrow the scope of rights for individuals and generate greater judicial deference to the legislative and executive branches of government. In both cases, the Court split over key issues and thereby illustrated that a new balance of power was tipping the Court's decisions in a particular direction but no consensus had yet been achieved among the justices on these issues.

Excessive Punishments

Ronald Harmelin was convicted of possessing 672 grams of cocaine in Michigan. He was not convicted of selling cocaine or of intending to distribute cocaine. Under that state's tough drug laws, he was given a mandatory sentence of life in prison without possibility of parole because he possessed more than 650 grams. Because Michigan had not had the death penalty since the 1840s, Harmelin's sentence represented the harshest possible punishment permitted for any offense under the state's laws. Even Michigan's convicted murderers tended to receive sentences that were for a term of years or a life sentence with the possibility of parole. Harmelin claimed that his sentence was "cruel and unusual" because it was disproportionate to the crime and because the sentencing statute did not permit a judge to take account of the individual circumstances in each case, such as the defendant's prior criminal record or lack thereof. Harmelin, for example, had no prior felony convictions on his record (*Harmelin v. Michigan* 1991, 994), yet he received the most severe punishment possible.

Writing on behalf of Chief Justice Rehnquist and Justices Kennedy, O'Connor, and Souter, Scalia rejected Harmelin's Eighth Amendment claims and declared that "[s]evere, mandatory penalties may be cruel, but they are not unusual in the constitutional sense, having been employed in various forms throughout our Nation's history" (ibid.). In emphasizing the original intentions of the Framers as the basis for his decision, Scalia noted that because mandatory death sentences were common when the Bill of Rights was drafted, the lesser sanction of mandatory life sentences could not be considered cruel and unusual (ibid., 995). Scalia also rejected Harmelin's argument that the Eighth Amendment mandates individualized sentencing by noting that the Supreme Court had required individualized attention to aggravating and mitigating factors only in death penalty cases (ibid.).

In other sections of his opinion, Scalia was joined only by Chief Justice Rehnquist. Scalia used these sections to lay the groundwork for what he hoped would be the eventual abolition of any proportionality requirement in the Eighth Amendment. In arguing against a proportionality requirement, Scalia asserted that because *Solem v. Helm*, concerning South Dakota's mandatory life sentences without parole for repeat offenders, was a 5-to-4 decision, the Court was not bound to adhere to the conclusions and reasoning of that precedent. According to Scalia (ibid., 965):

> It should be apparent...that our 5-to-4 decision eight years ago in *Solem* was scarcely the expression of clear and well accepted constitutional law. We have long recognized, of course, that the doctrine of *stare decisis* is less rigid in its application of constitutional precedents....Accordingly, we have addressed anew, and in greater detail, the question whether the Eighth Amendment contains a proportionality guarantee.... We conclude from this examination that *Solem* was simply wrong; the Eighth Amendment contains no proportionality guarantee.

Scalia justified the advancement of his anti-proportionality analysis by noting that the Court was deeply divided in deciding *Solem*. In reality, however, the Court was not deeply divided about the existence of a proportionality requirement in *Solem*, but merely about the application of that requirement to the facts in the case. The implication that the *Solem* decision cried out for reanalysis of the existence of a proportionality requirement was a misleading but useful justification for Scalia's opportunity to set out his views in hopes that justices in a future decision would discover and adopt his arguments. As a strategic matter, he gave his minority viewpoint on the existence of proportionality unusual prominence and visibility by discussing these arguments in sections I, II, III, and IV of his opinion before delivering the Court majority's decision in section V. Scalia was fortunate that the justice who agreed with his views on the existence of a proportionality requirement was Chief Justice Rehnquist. As chief justice, Rehnquist was able to use his power to assign majority-opinion responsibilities in a manner that permitted Scalia to reach a broad audience in the news media, academia, and legal community by writing the opinion which included, as a minor component, the Court's actual decision in Harmelin's closely-watched case. Even though a larger number of justices in the majority (Kennedy, O'Connor, and Souter) agreed with the four dissenters about the existence of a proportionality requirement in the Eighth Amendment, their views were less visible and prominent to commentators because they were expressed in a concurring opinion.

Scalia based the argument against the existence of a proportionality requirement on his historical analysis of the original meaning of the Eighth Amendment's prohibition against cruel and unusual punishments. Scalia argued that since the drafters of the Eighth Amendment were familiar with the concept of proportionate punishments but did not place language in the text to limit government to the use of such punishments, then no such constitutional guarantee existed (ibid., 974). In examining English objections to punishments imposed in seventeenth-century England, which provided the roots of the American Eighth Amendment, Scalia argued that the objections concerned the legality of English judges' activities in creating and imposing punishments, not the proportionality of those punishments (ibid., 973).

Significant debates surround the desirability and feasibility of using the Constitution's putative "original intent" as the basis for contemporary interpretation. There are disagreements about what the Framers of the Constitution originally intended with respect to each provision. Historical sources are incomplete and sometimes contradictory. Moreover, the document is filled with ambiguous phrases which are probably the result of compromises when there was no consensus about precise meaning even among those who drafted the language. There are also debates about *whose* intentions should be authoritative: the authors of each provision or the people whose ratification votes effectuated those provisions? In addition, there are questions about whether twentieth-century Americans should be bound by the understandings of their eighteenth-century forebears whose ideas were grounded in a vastly different social reality. Ultimately, interpretation by original intent has often been used as a means to justify individual justice's preferred policy outcomes. It has been employed selectively when useful and ignored when favorable to opponents' arguments (Macedo 1987; Smith 1989). Scalia frequently advocates interpretation by original intent, as he did when examining proportionality, but he is not consistently committed to this interpretive approach (Schultz and Smith 1996).

Scalia concluded his argument with an examination of precedents. He argued that although the *Weems* case made reference to proportionality of punishments, it was also based on the cruelly unusual nature of the punishment. In addition, he argued that federal courts did not engage in analysis of proportionality issues until the 1970s and that the U.S. Supreme Court focused its proportionality analysis only on death penalty cases. Thus Scalia argued that proportionality protection under the Eighth Amendment should be limited to capital cases which are treated with greater scrutiny and care by courts in several respects (*Harmelin v. Michigan* 1991, 994).

Scalia's opinion raised certain questions about his ultimate objectives. He concluded section I-A of the opinion with the categorical declaration that "the Eighth Amendment contains no proportionality requirement" (ibid., 965). At the conclusion of section IV, however, Scalia says that "[p]roportionality review is one of several respects in which we have held that 'death is different,' and have imposed protections that the Constitution nowhere else provides....We would leave [proportionality review for capital punishment], but will not extend it further" (ibid., 994). Because Scalia's historical analysis is presented to support his initial categorical conclusion, his acceptance of proportionality protection in death penalty cases appears to be a concession to the opposition. This concession seems designed to make more palatable Scalia's analysis which, hypothetically, could justify the use of capital punishment for minor offenses. Was this merely a temporary concession in a planned strategy to shrink the Eighth Amendment in a manner that would let states freely choose punishments to be imposed? Because Scalia's general philosophical approach is to leave public policies to "be defined by the majority through political processes" (Brisbin 1990, 27), Scalia may very well believe that electoral processes can be trusted to appropriately regulate the application of capital punishment within each state in accordance with the general historical principles of the Eighth Amendment.

Alternatively, Scalia may actually believe that capital punishment should be treated differently than other kinds of punishment. Two years before the *Harmelin* case, Scalia gave an address to a law school audience which indicated that he was personally uncomfortable with some of the implications of his own historical analysis of the Eighth Amendment's meaning. According to Scalia (1989, 864),

> What if some state should enact a new law providing public lashing, or branding of the right hand, as punishment for certain criminal offenses? Even if it could be demonstrated unequivocally that these were not cruel and unusual measures in 1791, and even though no prior Supreme Court decision has specifically disapproved them, I doubt whether any federal judge--even among the many who consider themselves originalists--would sustain them against an [E]ighth Amendment challenge....I am confident that public flogging and handbranding would not be

sustained by our courts, and any espousal of originalism as a practical theory of exegesis must somehow come to terms with that reality....I hasten to confess that in a crunch I may prove a faint-hearted originalist. I cannot imagine myself, any more than any other federal judge, upholding a statute that imposes the punishment of flogging.

Given Scalia's admitted rejection of the principles of original intent applied to their logical conclusion with respect to certain forms of criminal punishment, how can he conclude so emphatically that original intent principles must be strictly obeyed in the context of the Eighth Amendment's proportionality requirement? Moreover, if, as Scalia claims, the framers intended that there be no proportionality requirement, how can Scalia accept such a requirement for capital cases? If the requirement applies to capital cases, then why not apply it to other cases, too? When a justice purports to adhere to the mandates of clearly defined principles, evidence of that justice's simultaneous deviation from those principles creates the inference that the putative principles are merely rationalizations for the justice's preferred policy outcomes. In this instance, Scalia appeared intent upon shrinking the scope of the Eighth Amendment through selective application of an original intent approach to constitutional interpretation.

Scalia's discussion of the proportionality issue raised questions about the justice's acceptance of precedents that were not even discussed in his opinion. Most importantly, Scalia's reliance on an original intent approach to constitutional interpretation clashed with the Supreme Court's established method for defining cruel and unusual punishments. Since the *Trop v. Dulles* decision in 1958, the Court had defined the Eighth Amendment according to "evolving standards of decency that mark the progress of a maturing society" (*Trop v. Dulles* 1958, 101). In subsequent cases over more than three decades, the Court continued to use this formulation emphasizing contemporary societal values. Thus Scalia's advocacy for a static, historical basis for defining the constitutionality of punishments did not merely challenge the protection against disproportionate sentences; it implicitly clashed with additional Supreme Court precedents concerning the appropriate method for defining Eighth Amendment rights. Any eventual adoption of Scalia's approach by the Supreme Court would have dramatic impacts upon individuals' rights by significantly shrinking the scope of Eighth Amendment protections.

The *Harmelin* decision indicated that a majority of justices on the Supreme Court were inclined to defer to states' decisions about appropriate punishments whenever possible. Although only four justices saw Harmelin's punishment as disproportionate to his crime, seven justices still believed that the Eighth Amendment contained proportionality limits on punishment. However, three of the four justices who were most willing to scrutinize state sentencing decisions, White, Marshall, and Blackmun, retired within three years after the decision. Marshall's replacement, Clarence Thomas, quickly indicated that he shared Scalia's historical approach to the interpretation of the Eighth Amendment (Smith 1995a), and Blackmun's successor, Ruth Bader Ginsburg, demonstrated that she was less inclined than her predecessor to support individuals' rights in many issues (Smith, Baugh, Hensley, and Johnson 1994). Although Scalia's approach had not gained majority support, the retirements subsequent to *Harmelin* gave him an additional strong supporter and diluted the strength of the justices opposed to his conclusions about the Eighth Amendment's proportionality requirement. By characterizing precedents in a favorable fashion and selecting interpretive approaches that advanced his policy preferences, Scalia had previously proven his ability to successfully gain majority support for significant changes in constitutional doctrine when he rewrote and thereby limited restrictions on governmental impediments to the free exercise of religion (*Employment Division of Oregon v. Smith* 1990). Scalia's opinion in *Harmelin* set the stage for similar dramatic changes affecting the Eighth Amendment if the Court's composition were to change further in Scalia's favor.

The Supreme Court's deference to Michigan's cocaine statute did not mean that the Court would defer to government in every instance in which the severity of a sentencing decision was challenged. The *Harmelin* decision left open the question of precisely which punishments could garner majority support for the recognition of a disproportionate sentence. However, the Court subsequently expanded the potential Eighth Amendment protections for individuals by using the Excessive Fines Clause. In *Austin v. United States* (1993), an offender convicted of one count of possessing cocaine with intent to distribute challenged the forfeiture of his mobile home and auto body shop as a violation of the Eighth Amendment's prohibition against excessive fines. A unanimous Court found that forfeitures implicate the Eighth Amendment and remanded the case to the lower courts for a determination about whether the Excessive Fines Clause had been violated.

To an outside observer unfamiliar with the details of the Constitution, it might seem odd that justices who argued that there is no proportionality requirement with respect to the incarceration of offenders would later say that forfeiture of money and property could be unconstitutionally excessive. Which priority is more important and has a greater impact on human lives: loss of freedom or loss of property? For justices, such as Scalia, Rehnquist, and Thomas, who do not recognize a proportionality requirement, the decision can be explained in two ways. First, the Eighth Amendment's text contains a specific prohibition on excessive fines while it contains no reference to proportionality for other kinds of punishment (except bail, which is not really considered formal punishment). Second, Scalia, Thomas, and Rehnquist had been leaders on the Court in a series of divisive cases that ultimately provided greater constitutional protection for people's property (*Lucas v. South Carolina Coastal Commission* 1992; *Dolan v. City of Tigard* 1994). Thus protection of property from improper forfeiture was consistent with their conceptions of important constitutional rights deserving of judicial protection. The outcome of the case provided potentially broader protections for individuals by recognizing a governmental activity, forfeitures related to criminal cases, that could be limited by the Eighth Amendment. However, the expansion of this protection was not a harbinger of increased judicial surveillance of other kinds of punishment because several justices were motivated to protect property by textualist and policy-driven values that they did not apply to the incarceration of offenders for other offenses.

Interestingly, while the Court manifested property rights concerns about forfeiture as a potentially excessive fine, the conservative justices showed little such concern for the due process rights of innocent spouses whose husbands or wives use and forfeit family property while undertaking criminal activity (*Bennis v. Michigan* 1996).

Prison Conditions

The second significant decision of 1991, *Wilson v. Seiter*, was a unanimous decision with respect to the case outcome, but a 5-to-4 split with respect to the standard of review to be applied in prison conditions cases. As in the *Harmelin* case, it was Justices White, Blackmun, Marshall, and Stevens who disagreed with the direction in which Scalia sought to steer legal doctrine and public policy. In this case, however, Scalia was more successful in gaining the support of a majority for his reasoning and the subsequent retirements of White, Blackmun, and Marshall further weakened the opposition to Scalia's approach.

Pearly Wilson was a prisoner at the Hocking Correctional Facility, a state prison in Nelsonville, Ohio. He filed a civil rights action against Ohio corrections officials alleging that conditions at his prison violated the Eighth Amendment prohibition on cruel and unusual punishment. Wilson's lawsuit made a number of allegations: overcrowding; excessive noise; insufficient locker storage space; inadequate heating and cooling; improper ventilation; unclean and inadequate restrooms; unsanitary dining facilities and food preparation; and housing that mixed all prisoners with mentally and physically ill prisoners. Wilson sought judicial orders to correct the prison's alleged deficiencies. He also wanted to receive monetary damages totalling $900,000 for the alleged violations of his rights. The lower federal courts granted a summary judgment in favor of Ohio and the Supreme Court reviewed the case to determine whether the lower courts had made a proper decision.

In his majority opinion, Scalia traced his interpretation of the history of the Supreme Court's relevant Eighth Amendment decisions. He noted that *Estelle v. Gamble* (1976), concerning the alleged deprivation of medical care for prisoners, was the case in which the Supreme Court "first acknowledged that the [cruel and unusual punishment] provision could be applied to deprivations that were not specifically part of the sentence but were suffered during imprisonment." He noted that *Estelle* required prisoners to show that the deprivation of medical care was due to "deliberate indifference" and not merely to inadvertence or negligence. He noted that *Estelle*'s rule relied on the earlier death penalty case of *Louisiana ex rel. Francis v. Resweber* (1947), concerning a condemned offender who sought to avoid a second scheduled execution after the first execution attempt only shocked him in a nonfatal manner because of a faulty electric chair. Scalia quoted the justices who rejected Francis's claim as emphasizing that only the "wanton infliction of pain," with its implications for a culpable state of mind on the part of officials, rather than accidental equipment malfunctions, could come under the protections of the Eighth Amendment.

Scalia's review then skipped forward to *Rhodes v. Chapman* (1981), in which the Court had rejected a claim that double-celling constituted cruel and unusual punishment. Scalia argued that while the *Rhodes* decision was based on an objective evaluation of prison conditions, the Court later emphasized the subjective state of mind of prison officials in *Whitley v. Albers* (1986), just as they had emphasized subjective tests in *Estelle* and *Louisiana ex rel. Francis*. In *Whitley*, the Court required that a prisoner who was shot during an uprising show that the shooting was malicious and sadistic in order to demonstrate a violation of the Eighth Amendment's prohibition on cruel and unusual punishments.

The purpose of Scalia's review of these particular cases was to emphasize the Court's putative position that an intent requirement exists in the Eighth Amendment which forces prisoners to offer proof about corrections officials' state of mind as a cause of challenged prison conditions. It is not sufficient to show that prison conditions are terrible; the prisoner must also show that corrections officials were deliberately indifferent to the development of those conditions.

In reaching this conclusion, the Court rejected arguments made by the Bush administration on behalf of Wilson in which the United States government argued that the intent requirement should only apply to one-time problems, such as a malfunction in a heating system during the winter. In such instances, a rights violation would be recognized only if officials were deliberately indifferent to a problem that threatens prisoners' health and well-being. The U.S. government argued that, by contrast, continuing or systemic problems in prison conditions should be given judicial recognition and remedied no matter what prison officials were thinking. To do otherwise, according to the federal government, would allow prison officials to permit terrible conditions to develop but avoid responsibility and remediation by claiming that the officials were concerned about the problems but lacked the necessary funds to correct them.

Scalia's opinion rejected these arguments by claiming, first, that the word "punishment" in the Eighth Amendment necessarily referred only to actions taken by officials with some level of intention. According to Scalia, "If the pain inflicted is not formally meted out as *punishment* by the statute or the sentencing judge, some mental element must be attributable to the inflicting officer before [the hardship experienced by the prisoner] can qualify [as punishment under the Eighth Amendment]" (*Wilson v. Seiter* 1991, 300). Moreover, Scalia was unpersuaded by arguments about an intent requirement providing a basis for officials to avoid judicial scrutiny and supervision of prison conditions. According to Scalia, the Eighth Amendment's meaning and interpretation must be guided by consistent principles and not by the likely human consequences that would follow from applying a particular rule to different circumstances. In Scalia's words, "[e]ven if [it] were so [that officials could avoid judicial scrutiny by claiming a lack of funds to correct conditions], it is hard to understand how it could control the meaning of 'cruel and unusual punishment' in the Eighth Amendment. An intent requirement is either implicit in the word 'punishment' or is not; it cannot be alternately required and ignored as policy considerations might dictate" (ibid., 301).

As a matter of idealistic legal interpretation, Scalia's assertion makes sense. However, in the real world of Supreme Court decision making, the Court frequently takes different approaches to different kinds of cases. For example, the First Amendment makes the categorical assertion that "Congress shall make no law...abridging the freedom of speech," yet the Court's decisions have approved situational restrictions on speech under the rubric of reasonable time, place, and manner regulations. Scalia, for example, joined the majority that upheld a ban on soliciting at government-run airports (*International Society for Krishna Consciousness v. Lee* 1992). Moreover, at the very same time that Scalia drafted his *Wilson* opinion asserting that Eighth Amendment principles must be strictly adhered to, he also wrote the *Harmelin* opinion in which he applied his anti-proportionality analysis to non-capital punishments but not to capital punishment. Scalia's decision to stand on supposedly consistent principles without regard to contexts or consequences in the *Wilson* case appears to be a strategy to advance his preferred policy outcome: the reduction of the scope of Eighth Amendment protections for convicted offenders. His assertion of categorical principles sounds logical when presented in the *Wilson* opinion, but it does not withstand scrutiny when its selective application becomes evident through examination of other constitutional doctrines as well as Scalia's own interpretation of the Eighth Amendment in *Harmelin*.

In his *Wilson* opinion, Scalia sought to further limit the reach of the Eighth Amendment by asserting that general conditions in a prison can never violate the Eighth Amendment. According to Scalia, "*Some* conditions of confinement may establish an Eighth Amendment violation 'in combination' when each would not do so alone, but only when they have a mutually enforcing effect that produces the deprivation of a single, identifiable human need such as food, warmth, or exercise" (*Wilson v. Seiter* 1991, 304). This assertion apparently sought to limit the potential reach of the "totality of circumstances" test applied by some justices in examining conditions of confinement (*Rhodes v. Chapman* 1981, 363). By seeking to require findings of specific constitutional violations, Scalia could preempt future lower court decisions identifying Eighth Amendment violations for general conditions within a prison.

While the four justices who declined to join Scalia's opinion agreed that Wilson's case should be remanded, they objected to his analysis and conclusions about how such claims were to be evaluated. In a concurring opinion by Justice White, these justices noted that Scalia's interpretation of cases had not examined "those cases involv[ing] a challenge to conditions of confinement. Instead, [Scalia's selected cases] involved challenges to specific acts or omissions directed at individual prisoners" (*Wilson v. Seiter* 1991, 309), a situation different from that in *Wilson*. Scalia's review of precedents had included a case on medical care, the death penalty, double celling, and the shooting of a prisoner, none of which concerned general conditions of confinement as in *Wilson*. Most notably, Scalia omitted discussion of *Hutto v. Finney* (1978) in which the Supreme Court examined a case concerning unconstitutional conditions in an Arkansas prison. According to White, the justices focused only on objective conditions of confinement in that case and did not apply the subjective test of examining corrections officials' intentions. White's opinion also quoted other cases to indicate that, contrary to Scalia's doctrinal history, the emphasis on officials' subjective intent is not required by prior cases. According to White (*Wilson v. Seiter* 1991, 310),

> Not only is the majority's intent requirement a departure from precedent, it likely will prove impossible to apply in many cases. Inhuman prison conditions often are the result of cumulative actions and inactions by numerous officials inside and outside a prison, sometimes over a long period of time. In those circumstances, it is far from clear whose intent should be examined, and the majority offers no real guidance on this issue. In truth, intent is not very meaningful when considering a challenge to an institution, such as a prison system.

The concurring opinion raised concerns that "prison officials will be able to defeat a [civil rights lawsuit]....simply by saying that the conditions are caused by insufficient funding from the state legislature, rather than by any deliberate indifference on the part of prison officials" (ibid., 311). White's opinion concluded by raising the concern that "[t]he ultimate result of today's decision, I fear, is that 'serious deprivations of human needs,'...will go unredressed due to an unnecessary and meaningless search for 'deliberate indifference'" (ibid.).

White was correct in noting that Scalia's opinion had explicitly invited corrections officials to defend the conditions within their institutions, not by claiming that the conditions meet the humane standards previously thought to have been required by the Eighth Amendment but by merely claiming that they were helpless to remedy the conditions. In effect, the Eighth Amendment was changed from protecting prisoners against inhumane conditions to merely protecting prisoners from such conditions only when officials were "deliberately indifferent" to the conditions. White's concluding warning about the ineffectiveness of the Court's new test and the distracting nature of the search for improper intent implicitly presumed that his colleagues were concerned about protecting prisoners against the development of inhumane conditions within correctional institutions. As Scalia revealed in subsequent case decisions, he was not naively assuming that prisoners could actually be protected by his new standard. He was actually seeking to remove all judicial protections for inmates in correctional institutions. Just as Scalia failed to gain complete majority support for his rewriting of the proportionality requirement in *Harmelin*, he similarly failed to gain majority support when he revealed his true objectives in cases following the *Wilson* case. However, *Wilson* was decided before Scalia fully revealed his agenda and his ability to gain the bare-minimum, five-member majority in *Wilson* permitted him to take a significant stride toward his goal of blocking prisoners' civil rights suits alleging unconstitutional conditions. Scalia's victory was apparently attributable to his ability to characterize precedents persuasively in a fashion that favored his preferred outcomes and to his failure to reveal his true objectives to his fellow justices.

Less than one year after the *Wilson* decision, the Court addressed an important prison case in *Hudson v. McMillian* (1992). Keith Hudson was a prisoner in the state penitentiary at Angola, Louisiana. Hudson argued with corrections officer Jack McMillian and was thereupon placed in handcuffs and leg shackles and taken to the administrative lockdown section of the prison by McMillian and Officer Marvin Woods. According to Hudson, as he was being walked to the punishment section, "McMillian punched Hudson in the mouth, eyes, chest, and stomach while Woods held the inmate in place and kicked and punched him from behind" (*Hudson v. McMillian* 1992, 4). Arthur Mezo, the correctional supervisor, saw the beating being administered to Hudson and he merely told McMillian and Woods "not to have too much fun" (ibid.). As a result of the beating, Hudson suffered from minor bruises and swelling of his face, mouth, and lip as well as loosened teeth and a cracked partial dental plate, which was rendered unusable for several months.

Hudson sued for violation of his Eighth Amendment right against cruel and unusual punishments and he was awarded $800 by the federal district court. The federal court of appeals reversed the judgment. Although the appellate court found that the use of force was unreasonable, it said that a valid Eighth Amendment claim for such a beating could only be recognized if the inmate suffered from "significant injury," but Hudson's injuries were labeled as merely "minor." The Supreme Court accepted the case to determine whether the appellate court's "significant injury" requirement was actually mandated by the Eighth Amendment.

In a 7-to-2 opinion written by Justice Sandra O'Connor, the Court found that the Eighth Amendment does not require an inmate to suffer from a "significant injury" before initiating a valid lawsuit under such circumstances. The majority opinion accepted the *Wilson* requirement of evaluating the subjective intent of corrections officials. Here the Court found the requirement fulfilled because of the wanton and unnecessary use of force to inflict pain on the inmate. Much of the Court's opinion, however, was aimed at reinforcing and preserving the objective component of Eighth Amendment analysis, namely the nature of the harm to the prisoner. The Court declined to endorse the "significant injury" requirement which would have established a high standard for demonstrating harm. Instead, O'Connor emphasized that the Court was still applying "contemporary standards of decency" as the test for Eighth Amendment harms and recognized that even less serious harms can violate that standard. According to O'Connor (ibid., 9),

> When prison officials maliciously and sadistically use force to cause harm contemporary standards of decency always are violated....This is true whether or not significant injury is evident. Otherwise, the Eighth Amendment would permit any physical punishment, no matter how diabolic or inhuman, inflicting less than some arbitrary quantity of injury. Such a result would have been unacceptable to the drafters of the Eighth Amendment as it is today.

Thus the majority preserved the *Wilson* decision but limited its potential consequences by emphasizing that objective considerations of harm to prisoners must be considered and be considered flexibly along with the state of mind of the offending officials.

The two dissenters in the case were Justices Scalia and Thomas. In an opinion by Thomas, these two justices gave their first explicit indication that they actually believe that the Eighth Amendment should not be applied at all to protect prisoners against inhumane treatment or conditions in correctional institutions. Relying on the same kind of historical analysis concerned with the original intent of the Eighth Amendment's drafters that had been applied by Scalia in *Harmelin*,

Thomas argued that the Amendment was not intended to apply to protect prisoners:

> Surely prison was not a more congenial place in the early years of the Republic than it is today; nor were our judges and commentators so naive as to be unaware of the often harsh conditions of prison life. Rather, they simply did not conceive of the Eighth Amendment as protecting inmates from harsh treatment. Thus, historically, the lower courts routinely rejected prisoner grievances by explaining that the courts had no role in regulating prison life....It was not until 1976--185 years after the Eighth Amendment was adopted--that this Court first applied it to a prisoner's complaint about a deprivation suffered in prison.

Although Thomas may be correct about the Framers' lack of concern for incarcerated people at the time that they wrote the Eighth Amendment, his historical justification is suspect because prisons were not used for "punishment," the central focus of the Eighth Amendment, until the nineteenth century. According to Lawrence Friedman (1993, 77), prior to the nineteenth century, "jail was essentially a place to hold people for trial who could not make bail, and for debtors who could not pay debts." At the time that the Eighth Amendment was drafted and ratified at the end of the eighteenth century, criminal punishment primarily consisted of physical, non-incarcerative punishments, such as hanging, whipping, and the stocks. Moreover, because the Framers of the Eighth Amendment originally intended for it to apply only against the federal government, it is highly unlikely that they gave much thought at all to the conditions in jails, since those were essentially under state and local administration. Did the Framers intend to exclude prison conditions from Eighth Amendment coverage or did they simply not think about the issue at all because prisons had yet to come into widespread usage as a form of punishment? Thomas implies that the former is the case, but it seems more realistic to presume the latter. Thus Thomas's historical justification is less persuasive than it may appear.

Thomas's analysis implicitly advocates a return to the "hands-off" doctrine which characterized federal judicial review of prisoner cases prior to the 1960s. The "hands-off" doctrine had produced prisons containing horrific conditions in which prisoners were tortured, malnourished, and even murdered, yet Thomas and Scalia viewed judicial deference to correctional officials as the proper interpretation of the Eighth Amendment (Berkson 1975). The dissenters confirmed their deferential posture toward corrections officials by concluding their opinion with a sarcastic criticism of their colleagues' approach (*Hudson v. McMillian* 1992, 28):

> Today's expansion of the Cruel and Unusual Punishment Clause beyond all bounds of history and precedent is, I suspect, yet another manifestation of the pervasive view that the Federal Constitution must address all ills in our society. Abusive behavior by prison guards is deplorable conduct that properly evokes outrage and contempt. But that does not mean that it is invariably unconstitutional. The Eighth Amendment is not, and should not be turned into, a National Code of Prison Regulation.... [P]rimary responsibility for preventing and punishing [improper conduct by corrections officials] rests not with the Federal Constitution but with the laws and regulations of the various States.

Ironically, the dissenters' condemnations of their colleagues as misguided judicial activists targeted such stalwart conservatives as Chief Justice Rehnquist and Justices White, O'Connor, and Kennedy, all of whom regularly supported local criminal justice officials by declining to recognize defendants' and prisoners' rights in many contexts. The 7-to-2 vote in the *Hudson* case was more revealing about the extremism of Scalia and Thomas than about any liberal activism on the part of the other justices. The *Hudson* decision merely inhibited the restrictive potential of the *Wilson* decision. Because it was in the context of obviously intentional misconduct by corrections officials, it did not eliminate or reduce *Wilson*'s onerous burden on prisoners of proving the corrections officials' state of mind. However, because the decision clashed with Scalia's and Thomas's now-evident goal of eliminating Eighth Amendment protections for prisoners, the dissenters condemned the decision as if it had broken new ground and broadly expanded rights for inmates.

One year later in *Helling v. McKinney* (1993), the Supreme Court's seven-member majority renewed its commitment to preserving Eighth Amendment protections for prisoners as Scalia and Thomas reconfirmed their objective of eliminating Eighth Amendment protections for inmates. William McKinney was an inmate in the Nevada State Prison in Carson City. He was assigned to share a small cell with another inmate who smoked five packs of cigarettes each day. McKinney sued prison officials for threatening his health by forcing him into continuous exposure to second-hand smoke or, as the Supreme Court called it, "environmental tobacco smoke" (ETS). Prison officials argued that McKinney could not present a valid Eighth Amendment claim unless he could prove that he had suffered from serious medical problems caused by exposure to ETS. In effect, they claimed that the Amendment does not protect against prison conditions that threaten to cause future health problems.

In a majority opinion by Justice White, the Supreme Court rejected the contentions of the prison officials. According to White (*Helling v. McKinney* 1993, 25),

> We have great difficulty agreeing that prison authorities may not be deliberately indifferent to an inmate's current health problems but may ignore a condition of confinement that is sure or very likely to cause serious illness and needless suffering the next week or month or year....We would think that a prison inmate also could successfully complain about demonstrably unsafe drinking water without waiting for any attack of dysentery. Nor can we hold that prison officials may be deliberately indifferent to the exposure of inmates to a serious communicable disease on the grounds that the complaining inmate shows no serious current symptoms.

Although the Court did not use the example of AIDS, in an era in which communicable fatal illnesses are present in prison populations and society at large, it makes sense to recognize that prisoners would be left very vulnerable if they were required to show current injury as opposed to future potential harms. Again, the Court upheld the *Wilson* requirement of a showing of deliberate indifference as the state of mind of corrections officials. However, the *Helling* opinion preserved flexibility in the objective assessment of harms to prisoners by permitting the possibility of demonstrations of unreasonable risks instead of extant, concrete injuries.

Once again, Thomas and Scalia were the sole dissenters and in Thomas's dissenting opinion these justices applied their historical approach to argue more explicitly for the withdrawal of Eighth Amendment protections for prisoners. According to Thomas, "At the time the Eighth Amendment was ratified, the word 'punishment' referred to the penalty imposed for the commission of a crime....[Thus] I believe that the text and history of the Eighth Amendment, together with the decisions interpreting it, support the view that judges or juries but not jailers impose 'punishment'" (ibid., 38). To Thomas and

Scalia, the only definition of "punishment" and therefore the only applicability of the Eighth Amendment prohibition on cruel and unusual punishments concerned the sentencing decisions made by judges and not actions taken by corrections officials after the formal sentences had been pronounced.

The Court's approach to Eighth Amendment cases received further clarification in *Farmer v. Brennan* in 1994. Dee Farmer was serving a sentence in the federal prison system for credit card fraud. He had been diagnosed by medical personnel in the U.S. Bureau of Prisons as a "transsexual," an unusual psychiatric disorder in which people are uncomfortable with their anatomical gender. For several years prior to being convicted and imprisoned at age 18, Farmer wore women's clothing, underwent therapy with female hormones, received silicone breast implants, and submitted to a botched "black market" sex-change operation. He claimed to have received hormone treatments from drugs smuggled into the prison and prison officials agreed that his manner of dress and appearance projected "feminine characteristics" (*Farmer v. Brennan* 1994, 1975). Farmer served his time in several federal correctional institutions. Sometimes he was housed with the general population and at other times he was placed in segregation. He was segregated for disciplinary violations on some occasions, but at other times his segregation was based on a concern about his safety.

For disciplinary reasons, Farmer was transferred from a federal prison in Wisconsin to a federal prison with a higher security classification in Indiana. The Indiana prison contained more prisoners prone to violence or convicted of violent offenses. Two weeks after being placed in the general population at the Indiana prison, Farmer was beaten and raped by another inmate. Farmer filed a lawsuit against prison officials asserting that those officials transferred him to a dangerous, violent prison environment despite their knowledge that his feminine characteristics would make him especially vulnerable to violent sexual assaults by other inmates. Because Farmer did not prove that he had complained about the transfer or that prison officials had actual knowledge about the potential danger to him, the lower federal courts dismissed his case for failure to demonstrate the "deliberate indifference" standard required by *Wilson*.

The Supreme Court accepted the case in order to define how the subjective "deliberate indifference" standard should be applied. The Court unanimously decided to remand Farmer's case to the lower courts for further consideration. The majority opinion by Justice David Souter was joined by all of the justices except Thomas. The Court held that "a prison official cannot be found liable under the Eighth

Amendment for denying an inmate humane conditions of confinement unless the official knows of and disregards excessive risk to inmate health and safety; the official must both be aware of facts from which the inference could be drawn that a substantial risk of harm exists, and he must also draw the inference" (ibid., 1979). In setting this standard, the Court reiterated that mere negligence by corrections officials would not be sufficient to violate the Eighth Amendment. However, the Court also emphasized that prisoners need not prove the much higher standard of malicious acts that intentionally seek to harm the prisoner. Although the Court adopted a middle-ground standard for the subjective intent requirement of *Wilson*, the Court's definition of this "deliberate indifference" standard still posed substantial difficulties for prisoners seeking to prove unconstitutional conditions of confinement.

The *Farmer* decision precluded the worst-case scenario raised by dissenters in *Wilson* who feared that corrections officials could avoid liability by saying "We knew about the terrible conditions, but we did not have enough money to fix it." After *Farmer*, if prison officials knew about inhumane conditions, they would be liable for not implementing remedies. However, because of the continued existence of the subjective intent requirement from *Wilson* as well as *Farmer*'s definition of that requirement, corrections officials were still invited to seek to avoid liability by claiming ignorance about inhumane conditions.

Justices John Paul Stevens and Harry Blackmun wrote concurring opinions in which they continued to object, as they had since joining the dissent in *Wilson*, to the existence of any subjective intent requirement. To these two justices, inhumane conditions violated the Eighth Amendment whether or not the corrections officials were aware of those conditions. As a practical matter, these justices preferred a rule that would require officials to seek out and remedy inhumane conditions without the option of tolerating such conditions out of ignorance or claimed ignorance. In fact, Stevens had demonstrated his prescience by dissenting against the original formulation of the subjective intent standard in *Estelle v. Gamble* in 1976. It is no small irony that Justice Thurgood Marshall set out the subjective intent standard in the specific context of medical care in *Estelle* and then found himself objecting to that very standard fifteen years later after Scalia's opportunistic appropriation and expansion of the standard to prison conditions generally. Throughout the entire two decades of prison conditions cases, Stevens alone consistently maintained that "a state official may inflict cruel and unusual punishment without any improper subjective motivation" (ibid., 1989).

CONCLUSION

Consistent with its conservative composition, the Rehnquist Court has not strictly scrutinized criminal punishments and the constitutionality of conditions within the prisons. The Court deferred to a state's severe punishment standards in *Harmelin* and relaxed judicial supervision of prison conditions through imposition of a subjective intent test in *Wilson*. Moreover, even in those cases in which the Court was receptive to prisoners' arguments, such as *Hudson*, *Helling*, and *Farmer*, the Court's decisions merely permitted such cases to proceed in the judicial process and did not ensure that prisoners would prevail in such lawsuits.

Despite the conservatizing impact of Rehnquist Court decisions on the Eighth Amendment, the justices have not moved in lock-step fashion to eliminate constitutional protections for convicted offenders. Contrary to the Court's image and reputation in other areas affecting constitutional rights, the Rehnquist-era judicial decisions have explicitly preserved constitutional rights, albeit with a lower degree of protection, even when given the opportunity to shrink the Eighth Amendment more dramatically. The majority of justices have resisted calls from Scalia and Thomas to eliminate the proportionality requirement and to withdraw Eighth Amendment protections from incarcerated offenders. Even when establishing new standards that favor the government, such as *Wilson*'s subjective intent requirement, a majority of justices kept the new test from being taken to its most stringent conclusion by rejecting the serious injury requirement sought by officials in *Hudson*, permitting lawsuits for risks to health in *Helling* and establishing a mid-range test for subjective intent in *Farmer*.

Although the positions advocated by extreme conservatives found expression in the opinions of Scalia and Thomas, the other justices, including such consistent conservatives as Rehnquist and O'Connor, demonstrated that there is a relatively broad consensus among conservative and liberal justices in support of acknowledging Eighth Amendment protections covering criminal punishment and prison conditions. The level of protection and degree of supervision may be diminished from the prior years in which federal judges assertively took control over prison systems (Yackle 1989). However, this reduction in judicial intervention is not merely a result of the relaxed Eighth Amendment standards applied by the Rehnquist Court in *Wilson*. It is also a natural consequence of correctional improvements spurred by judicial decisions in the 1970s and 1980s as well as the increasing professionalization of correctional administrators (Feeley 1989). The

Rehnquist Court moved judges away from intervention in punishment issues, but it did not remove the judiciary entirely from this arena of legal and policy issues.

Although the Rehnquist Court left open avenues for judicial remedies when the newly raised standards for proving violations were met, Congress moved ahead in 1996 to impose further limitations on prisoners' ability to succeed in civil rights lawsuits over prison conditions. The Prison Litigation Reform Act of 1996, which was included as a relatively unnoticed component of omnibus budget reconciliation legislation, contained several new provisions favoring the interests of government officials ("New Law" 1996; Loven 1996). The law made it easier for states to end court supervision of their correctional institutions while it simultaneously made it more difficult for prisoners to file more than three constitutional claims, which is not necessarily a large number if one considers that many prisoners may be incarcerated for decades. While these legislative developments have, in some respects, created more limitations on prison reform litigation than those imposed by the Rehnquist Court, they have not made the Supreme Court irrelevant.

Decisions by the Court continue to affect whether and how prisoners will be able to make use of the remaining avenues to challenge allegedly unconstitutional conditions within prisons. Most notably, in 1996, the Rehnquist Court severely restricted the authority of lower court judges to impose system-wide remedies for deficiencies in the law libraries and legal assistance made available to prisoners. The Court's decision in *Lewis v. Casey* (1996) placed prisoners in a "catch-22" situation: in order to gain judicially ordered library or other assistance for the preparation of their legal petitions, they need have enough facility with literacy and legal procedure to demonstrate that available resources are insufficient to fulfill their constitutional right of access to the courts. In light of the Congress's actions to affect prison reform litigation, the Rehnquist Court's greatest impact on Eighth Amendment prison issues in the immediate future could actually stem from its decision affecting access to prison law libraries, which may make it difficult for many prisoners to bring forward Eighth Amendment claims, rather than from cases addressing punishment issues.

CHAPTER 3

The Ultimate Punishment: Discretion and Discrimination in the Death Penalty

The death penalty stands out among criminal punishments. The ultimate punishment is notable for its severity and finality. The penalty is not unique to the United States, but there are no other industrialized countries that retain capital punishment except for countries in the former Soviet bloc. Moreover, unlike with incarceration, mistakes made in the identification of offenders cannot be corrected after the punishment has been implemented. This ultimate punishment embodies the maximum deprivation of liberty and thereby challenges the American justice system to insure that due process and other constitutional rights are scrupulously protected.

The Supreme Court's most famous decisions concerning capital punishment were made during the Burger Court era. Joseph Hoffmann (1993, 147) looked back from the vantage point of the Rehnquist Court era when he wrote,

> Since [1976], the Court has not seriously reconsidered the claim that the death penalty itself violates the Eighth Amendment. And in light of the apparent nationwide increase in popular support for the death penalty during the 1980s, it is unlikely that a challenge to the constitutionality of the death penalty alone will attract the Court's attention in the near future.

Taken at face value, Hoffmann's statement could convey the impression that the major issues concerning the death penalty were settled prior to the beginning of the Rehnquist Court era. While this conclusion is arguably correct with respect to the fundamental question of capital punishment's constitutionality, the Rehnquist Court has, in fact, had a significant but not adequately recognized impact on the death penalty. The Burger Court's decisions about the permissibility of the death penalty have remained intact. However, the Rehnquist Court's decisions have broadened the applicability of capital punishment through a series of decisions that have expanded discretionary decision-making in capital cases and thereby increased risks of arbitrary, discriminatory, and erroneous decisions in death penalty cases.

THE BURGER COURT AND
THE CONSTITUTIONALITY OF CAPITAL PUNISHMENT

As Lee Epstein and Joseph Kobylka's (1992) careful study of capital punishment litigation in the U.S. Supreme Court explained in great detail, the high court struggled with the issue of the death penalty during the early 1970s. Capital punishment had fallen into disfavor within industrialized nations by the end of the 1960s. The United States was virtually alone among industrialized democracies in retaining the use of executions as a punishment for crime. Among industrialized countries, the communist nations of the Soviet bloc and apartheid-driven South Africa were the remaining nations which employed capital punishment, yet the United States normally did not wish to find itself in the company of such pariah states in the development and implementation of public policies concerning due process and justice. Social forces appeared to be moving against the death penalty as public opinion polls indicated more Americans opposed capital punishment than supported it in the mid-1960s, interest groups prepared new cases to challenge its constitutionality, and several state supreme courts struck down capital punishment laws in their own states (ibid., 47, 77).

As support for the death penalty diminished and opposition to the ultimate punishment grew, an informal moratorium on executions by the states set the stage for a clarifying decision by the Supreme Court concerning the permissibility of capital punishment. In 1972, the Supreme Court issued its decision in *Furman v. Georgia* (1972) and several companion cases in which the Legal Defense Fund (LDF) had argued that the death penalty was out of step with contemporary standards of decency which defined cruel and unusual punishment under the Eighth Amendment. LDF lawyers had also argued that the broad discretion given to judges and juries produced arbitrary decisions and discrimination. In a *per curiam* opinion, the Court declared that capital punishment *as then applied* violated the Eighth and Fourteenth Amendments. The Court's decision did not abolish the death penalty because the justices could not agree on a single rationale to justify their decision. Only two justices, Thurgood Marshall and William Brennan, forthrightly concluded that the death penalty was always unconstitutional because of its inherent conflict with the evolving contemporary standards that define the Eighth Amendment. Three other justices, William O. Douglas, Potter Stewart, and Byron White, concluded that capital punishment was being carried out in impermissible ways that produced arbitrariness and discrimination because of the broad discretion utilized by judges and juries in determining sentences. Four dissenting justices argued that capital punishment was constitutionally acceptable and Chief Justice Burger's opinion advised the states on how to write new death penalty statutes that might meet the Court's approval by limiting the scope of decisionmakers' discretion (Epstein and Kobylka 1992, 80).

In the aftermath of the *Furman* decision, Congress and the legislatures in many states drafted new capital punishment laws designed to address White's and Stewart's objections to the application of the death penalty prior to 1972. These new statutes sought to guide decisions in capital cases and thereby reduce the arbitrariness produced by excessive discretion. Thus the new statutes typically created bifurcated proceedings in which a hearing to consider punishment would be conducted separately after a determination of guilt had already been rendered. The creation of a separate punishment hearing to consider the possible imposition of the death penalty was intended to focus the judges' and jurors' attention solely on the issue of capital punishment and prevent any careless merging of decisions about culpability and punishment (ibid., 86). Legislatures also sought to inform jurors about which factors to focus upon and use in deciding whether a guilty defendant would receive the death penalty or a significant term of incarceration. In particular, the new laws emphasized consideration of aggravating factors, such as the prior record of the offender and any special viciousness in the criminal act, as the basis for imposing the death penalty. Some states also required consideration of mitigating factors, such as the youthfulness or mental state of the defendant, which might tend to weigh against the imposition of death (ibid). By focusing the judges' and jurors' attention on specified factors, these legislatures hoped that capital punishment could resume without any further concerns about the arbitrary imposition of death sentences.

The new death penalty statutes were tested in *Gregg v. Georgia* in 1976. Under Georgia's new law, Gregg was sentenced to death after a bifurcated proceeding in which the jury was required to find the existence of one or more statutorily specified aggravating factors before imposing the death penalty. In Gregg's case, an aggravating circumstance existed because the murder was committed during the course of an armed robbery. In a 7-to-2 decision, the Court endorsed Georgia's new statute and thereby reactivated the death penalty.

Justice Stewart's plurality opinion found that the procedural reforms in Georgia's statute satisfied the concerns raised in *Furman* (*Gregg v. Georgia* 1976, 206):

> The basic concern of *Furman* centered on those defendants who were being condemned to death capriciously and arbitrarily. Under the procedures before the Court in that case, sentencing authorities were not directed to give attention to the nature or circumstances of the crime committed or to the character or record of the defendant. Left unguided, juries imposed the death sentence in a way that could only be called freakish. The new Georgia sentencing procedures, by contrast, focus the jury's attention on the particularized nature of the crime and the particularized characteristics of the individual defendant.

In dissent, Justices Brennan and Marshall maintained their categorical opposition to the death penalty, but by this time their voting strength had been weakened by the retirement of Justice Douglas. Moreover, the *Gregg* decision made it clear that Justices Stewart and White had not opposed capital punishment in *Furman* but had merely objected to the procedures applied in such cases at that time.

On the same day that the *Gregg* decision was issued, the Court emphasized its commitment to individualized sentencing through its decision in *Woodson v. North Carolina* (1976). *Woodson* invalidated state statutes that imposed a mandatory death sentence in first-degree murder cases. Mandatory capital punishment clashed with *Gregg*'s emphasis on making judgments about the individual defendant and particular crime before determining whether to apply capital punishment. The Court further advanced its emphasis on individualized sentencing in *Lockett v. Ohio* (1978) by prohibiting states from barring consideration of mitigating factors in making the punishment decision in capital cases. As a result of these decisions, although defendants who commit similar crimes may receive different punishments based on different mitigating circumstances in each case, arbitrariness was presumed to be prevented by the judges' and juries' careful consideration of specified factors during the bifurcated proceedings (White 1991, 7).

DISCRIMINATION AND THE VALUE OF HUMAN LIVES

In its very first term, the Rehnquist Court tackled several cases concerning capital punishment (*Booth v. Maryland* 1987; *McCleskey v. Kemp* 1987; *Tison v. Arizona* 1987). In its most important case of 1987, the Court addressed the issue of racial discrimination in capital sentencing. Warren McCleskey, an African American man, was convicted and sentenced to death for killing a police officer during a furniture store robbery in Fulton County, Georgia. In challenging his sentence, McCleskey relied on a study conducted by Professors David Baldus, George Woodworth, and Charles Pulaski which came to be known as "the Baldus study." The researchers examined more than 2,000 murder cases in Georgia during the 1970s in order to evaluate the factors associated with the imposition of the death penalty. The study did not simply count the numbers of white and African American defendants who received the death penalty. Instead, the study used sophisticated statistical methods to examine whether a defendant's prior criminal record, the heinousness of the crime, or other factors determined the imposition of capital punishment. While taking account of 230 variables, the study found that race played an important role in determining which murder defendants would be sentenced to death. The race of the victim as well as the race of the defendant emerged as important factors in capital sentencing as the criminal justice system vindicated white victims and treated African American defendants most harshly. These results were consistent with findings from other states concerning arbitrariness and discrimination in capital sentencing (Nakell and Hardy 1987; Gross and Mauro 1984). As described by Justice Lewis Powell in the majority opinion (*McCleskey v. Kemp* 1987, 287):

> [Baldus] found that the death penalty was assessed in 22% of the cases involving black defendants and white victims; 8% of the cases involving white defendants and white victims; 1% of the cases involving black defendants and black victims; and 3% of the cases involving white defendants and black victims.

In a dissenting opinion, Justice Brennan stated the study's findings even more starkly in revealing the criminal justice system's placement of a higher value on whites' lives than on those of African Americans (ibid., 327):

> [B]lacks who kill whites are sentenced to death at nearly *22 times* the rate of blacks who kill blacks, and more than *7 times* the rate of whites who kill

blacks. In addition, prosecutors seek the death penalty for 70% of black defendants with white victims, but for only 15% of black defendants with black victims, and only 19% of white defendants with black victims....[Georgia] has executed 7 persons. All of the 7 were convicted of killing whites, and 6 of the 7 executed were black....[E]xecution figures are especially striking in light of the fact that, during the period encompassed by the Baldus study, only 9.2% of Georgia homicides involved black defendants and white victims, while 60.7% involved black victims.

Because of this evidence of systemic racial discrimination in Georgia's capital sentencing, the Court was faced with the question of whether capital punishment in that state violated the Equal Protection Clause of the Fourteenth Amendment. In a 5-to-4 decision, the Court concluded that there was no constitutional violation. Justice Powell's majority opinion rejected the use of statistics to demonstrate the existence of systemic discrimination affecting death penalty sentences. This conclusion placed Powell in the awkward position of explaining why the Court accepts statistics to show racial discrimination in employment discrimination cases and in jury selection, two categories of cases which presumably are less important than decisions about life and death. Powell's rationalization for rejecting statistics in capital cases rested on the claimed uniqueness of each criminal case and on the importance of discretion in criminal justice decision making. According to Powell, "Because discretion is essential to the criminal justice process, we would demand exceptionally clear proof before we would infer that the discretion has been abused" (ibid., 297). Powell's defense of discretionary decision making in criminal justice was a harbinger of the Rehnquist Court's ultimate legacy with respect to capital punishment. The Court's decisions, beginning with *McCleskey*, clearly signaled that the majority of justices were loath to interfere with states' choices about whom to execute and thereby facilitated an expansion in discretion and concomitant discrimination in applying capital punishment.

In examining McCleskey's claim that the Baldus study demonstrated that Georgia's capital punishment scheme violated the Eighth Amendment's prohibition on arbitrary and capricious death sentences, Powell belittled the use of statistics and exalted the importance of discretion in criminal justice decision making. Powell noted that statistics cannot "prove" the existence of racial discrimination, but merely "may show only a likelihood that a particular factor entered into some decisions" (ibid., 309). Powell's statement about statistics, while accurate as a general conclusion, did not account for the sophisticated methods of Baldus's detailed study and the impact that such sophistication has on the confidence that one can have in the "likelihood" of discrimination demonstrated by the study. As Justice Brennan noted in dissent (ibid., 327),

> McCleskey's statistics have particular force because most of them are the product of sophisticated multiple-regression analysis. Such analysis is designed precisely to identify patterns in the aggregate, even though we may not be able to reconstitute with certainty any individual decision that goes to make up that pattern. Multiple-regression analysis is particularly well-suited to identify the influence of impermissible considerations in sentencing since it is able to control for permissible factors that may explain an apparent arbitrary pattern.

Powell concluded that "[a]t most, the Baldus study indicates a discrepancy that appears to correlate with race. Apparent disparities in sentencing are an inevitable part of our criminal justice system" (ibid., 313). The difficulty with this conclusion is not merely that powerful, sophisticated statistical evidence had been reduced to the mere demonstration of a "discrepancy" but that Powell overlooked the constitutional prohibition on certain kinds of "discrepanc[ies]." The Constitution does not require equal treatment in all cases, but the Equal Protection Clause does forbid governmental racial discrimination in criminal sentencing. Racial "discrepancies" are not the same as other kinds of discrepancies because the right to equal protection is specifically and most strongly focused on the eradication of racial discrimination in governmental policies and practices.

In an analysis of the Court's *McCleskey* decision, Judge Julian Cook and Professor Mark Kende (1996) found that the justices were inconsistent in their treatment of equal protection issues. While the majority resisted recognizing the existence of unconstitutional racial discrimination affecting capital punishment, these same justices were much more accepting of less compelling claims when white voters alleged discrimination in the design of legislative districts (*Shaw v. Reno* 1993). Thus the *McCleskey* majority's apparent desire to preserve capital punishment in spite of strong evidence of racial discrimination does not appear grounded in a consistent application of equal protection doctrines.

Part of Justice Powell's reluctance to recognize the serious issue of racial discrimination presented by the Baldus study appeared to stem from evident concerns that a decision favorable to *McCleskey* would have a significant impact on criminal justice systems throughout the nation. Powell was apprehensive about disrupting the application of discretionary decision making in criminal justice. He declared that "Where the discretion that is so fundamental to our criminal process is involved, we decline to assume that what is unexplained is invidious" (*McCleskey v. Kemp* 1987, 313). Powell also admitted that his decision was guided, in part, by a concern that the recognition of racial discrimination in Georgia's capital sentencing would produce new cases alleging racial discrimination in other kinds of sentences in Georgia and elsewhere (ibid., 316). This did not appear to be a compelling consideration since the Court's entire post-*Furman* jurisprudence had treated capital cases differently than other kinds of cases with respect to the specific requirements of factors to be considered in individualized sentencing. Such differentiation between capital and non-capital cases was justified by the recognition that the death penalty is qualitatively different than other kinds of punishment and errors discovered in capital case decision making, unlike those in other cases, cannot be remedied after the sentence is implemented.

In his dissenting opinion, Justice Stevens alluded to Powell's rationalizations in concluding that "The Court's decision appears to be based on a fear that the acceptance of McCleskey's claim would sound the death knell for capital punishment in Georgia" (ibid., 367). Although the majority seemed to be doing everything it could to avoid treating seriously evidence that might force them to reduce the scope of capital punishment, Stevens noted that "[i]f society were indeed forced to choose between a racially discriminatory death penalty (one that provides heightened protection against murder "for whites only") and no death penalty at all, the choice mandated by the Constitution would be plain" (ibid.). Although Stevens believed that the Court should confront the strong evidence of racial discrimination rather than avoid it, he concluded that the majority was mistakenly fearful that a decision favoring McCleskey would effectively abolish the death penalty. Stevens believed that such a decision may narrow the category of cases eligible for capital punishment, but he did not share the majority's apparent fears that any acknowledgement of the existence of racial discrimination would automatically lead to the demise of a punishment that a majority of justices seemed determined to preserve.

The majority's rejection of sophisticated social science evidence was a discouraging blow against critics' hopes that the Supreme Court could think seriously about and realistically recognize the impact of its decisions upon people's lives. According to James Acker (1993, 81),

The prevailing opinions in the Court's recent major capital punishment decisions have increasingly displayed an unwillingness to incorporate the results of relevant social science findings. This trend has profound implications for developing death penalty doctrine....Unfettered by empirical evidence relating to capital punishment administration, a working majority of the justices has emphasized alternative priorities to guide death penalty decisions. These other objectives include....ensuring that procedures governing death penalty decisions are not so demanding as to jeopardize the states' ability to maintain viable capital punishment systems (*McCleskey v. Kemp*, 1987).

Did the majority of justices reject McCleskey's claim because they were more concerned about protecting the continued existence of capital punishment than upholding the constitutional prohibition against racial discrimination in criminal sentencing? As indicated in the foregoing discussion, the reasoning in Powell's majority opinion gives indications that the justices were straining to avoid any acknowledgement of racial discrimination that might limit the availability of the death penalty as a criminal punishment. Normally, the justices' opinions are the sole source of information about Supreme Court decisions and analysts must necessarily reach speculative conclusions by interpreting the justices' words and reasoning. In the *McCleskey* case, however, there is additional evidence that at least one justice, Antonin Scalia, decided that it was more important to preserve the availability of the death penalty than to stop racial discrimination.

In the late Justice Thurgood Marshall's papers in the Library of Congress, Professor Dennis Dorin discovered a memorandum that Scalia, a member of the majority, circulated to the other justices as they were deciding *McCleskey*. In the memorandum, Scalia forthrightly acknowledged the existence of racial discrimination (Dorin 1994). Unlike Powell, Scalia did not find fault with the evidence of discrimination presented in the Baldus study. According to Scalia's memorandum (1987),

I disagree with the argument that the inferences that can be drawn from the Baldus study are weakened by the fact that each jury and each trial is unique, or by the large number of variables at issue. And I do not share the view, implicit in [Powell's draft opinion], that an effect of racial factors upon sentencing, if it could be shown by sufficiently strong statistical evidence, would require reversal. Since it is my view that the unconscious operation of irrational sympathies and antipathies, including racial, upon jury decisions and (hence) prosecutorial [ones] is real, acknowledged by the [cases] of this court and ineradicable, I cannot honestly say that all I need is more proof. I expect to write separately on these points, but not until I see the dissent.

Contrary to the expectations raised by this memorandum, Scalia ultimately merely joined Powell's majority opinion without writing any opinion of his own. As a result, Scalia, whose vote was decisive within the five-member majority, permitted Warren McCleskey to be executed after acknowledging that McCleskey's sentence was the product of a sentencing system infused with racial bias. Unlike Powell, who sought to avoid acknowledging the demonstrated existence of racial discrimination because it would require ruling in McCleskey's favor Scalia "trivializ[ed] [racist practices] by saying, in a single-paragraph memo, that they were merely an unavoidable and legally unassailable, part of life for African-Americans" (Dorin, 1994, 1077). As Dorin has concluded, "Apparently for Scalia, the capital punishment system's valuing a white life significantly above a black one did not implicate any constitutional provisions" (ibid.).

While members of the *McCleskey* majority manifested different approaches to the issue of racial discrimination, with Powell declining to recognize the problem and Scalia refusing to remedy it, the net result was the same: states maintained their ability to impose capital punishment despite strong evidence of racial discrimination in its application.

During the Rehnquist Court's first term, the justices also considered a case involving the constitutionality of Victim Impact Statements during capital sentencing. Maryland's court procedures permitted murder victims' family members to speak to the jury about the loss caused by the murder defendants' actions. In a 5-to-4 decision in *Booth v. Maryland* (1987), the Supreme Court determined that Victim Impact Statements impermissibly "serve[d] no other purpose than to inflame the jury and divert it from deciding the case on the relevant evidence concerning the crime and the defendant" (*Booth v. Maryland* 1987, 508). The Court divided along precisely the same lines as the voting blocs in *McCleskey*, except that Justice Powell saw Victim

Impact Statements, unlike statistical proof of racial discrimination, as violating the Constitution. Thus Powell joined the four justices who dissented against his *McCleskey* decision to form the majority in *Booth*. The majority in *Booth* recognized that the use of Victim Impact Statements could lead death penalty decisions to hinge on perceptions of the victim's character rather than on the actions, intentions, and culpability of the defendant. Thus, such statements could increase the likelihood that capital punishment would be applied to avenge the deaths of prominent or otherwise highly valued citizens and thereby diminish the justice system's regard for other victims.

The Court revisited the issue two years later in *South Carolina v. Gathers* (1989). In *Gathers*, the prosecutor used the closing arguments to make victim impact comments to the jury about the victim's religious beliefs and patriotism. The Court's composition had changed since *Booth* because Powell had retired and been replaced by Justice Anthony Kennedy, who promptly joined Rehnquist, Scalia, and O'Connor in supporting the permissibility of Victim Impact Statements. However, Justice White, a dissenter in *Booth*, joined the majority because he believed that *Booth* dictated the outcome as the controlling precedent and that the Court could not permit the use of Victim Impact Statements without explicitly overruling *Booth*. In dissent, Scalia argued strongly that the Court should overturn *Booth*, even though the precedent had been set only two years earlier. Scalia argued that a quick reversal would not harm the Court's image as the institutional purveyor and guardian of stable legal principles (*South Carolina v. Gathers* 1989, 824). Moreover, Scalia explicitly alluded to the role of the Court's personnel changes in affecting the reversal of precedent: "Overrulings of precedent rarely occur without a change in the Court's personnel" (ibid.). This surprisingly frank admission about the role of a political process, namely the selection of new justices by the President, in determining legal doctrines seemed to indicate that Scalia looked forward to further personnel changes that might advance his preferred outcome. Shortly thereafter, Scalia's wish came true.

The retirement of Justice Brennan in 1990 brought to the Court a new Republican appointee, David Souter, whose initial performance as a justice showed him to be a strong supporter of the conservative bloc (Johnson and Smith 1992). Although Souter's decisions became more liberal in subsequent terms, he initially moved the Court in a conservative direction by providing the decisive vote in favor of conservative positions in several important criminal justice cases (Smith and Johnson 1992). Souter's presence on the Court helped to turn the tide in a new direction when the justices revisited the Victim Impact Statement issue for the third time in a brief six-year period.

In *Payne v. Tennessee* (1991), a murder victim's mother was permitted to testify about the impact of the murder on the victim's two-year-old son. Chief Justice Rehnquist's description of the case was particularly graphic, including the amount of blood that a young stabbing victim received in a transfusion during surgery and the police officers' description of the defendant as "wild...[and] foaming at the mouth" (*Payne v. Tennessee* 1991, 813). In overruling *Booth* and *Gathers*, Rehnquist emphasized that states ought to be able to determine what kinds of evidence jurors should consider in determining the defendant's blameworthiness. The majority opinion also expressed the view that information presented to the jury during the sentencing phase unfairly favored the defendant because the defendant could present mitigating evidence about his or her positive personal qualities but no evidence was permitted about the victims. Thus, contrary to the Supreme Court's usual slogans about the need to respect and adhere to case precedents, the new majority quickly reversed precedents that were only two and four years old respectively. According to Rehnquist, the Court's disregard for case precedent in this case was appropriate because "*Booth* and *Gathers* were decided by the narrowest of margins, over spirited dissents challenging the basic underpinnings of those decisions. They have been questioned by Members of the Court in later decisions and have defied consistent application by the lower courts" (ibid., 828). All of these factors may have been perfectly true, just as they are for other controversial cases, but Rehnquist would have been more forthright if he simply admitted that the Court's composition had changed and Souter's vote provided the needed impetus to move doctrines in a direction comporting with conservatives' preferences.

In dissent, Justice Marshall broadcast that which Rehnquist's majority opinion did not admit: "Neither the law nor the facts supporting *Booth* and *Gathers* underwent any change in the last four years. Only the personnel of this Court did" (ibid., 844). Both Marshall and Stevens, who wrote a separate dissent, emphasized that when Victim Impact Statements present information about victims that was unknown to the defendant and unconnected to any motive or action of the defendant, this information has no relevance to judgments about the defendant's blameworthiness. According to Stevens, "Our cases provide no support whatsoever for the majority's conclusion that the prosecutor may introduce evidence that sheds no light on the defendant's guilt or moral culpability, and thus serves no purpose other than to encourage jurors to decide in favor of death rather than life on the basis of their emotions rather than their reason" (ibid., 856). Stevens called the *Payne* decision "a sad day for a great institution" (ibid., 867) because he perceived that popular fears of crime and the victims' rights movement, both of which were central justifications for Scalia's opinions in *Booth* and *Payne*, had replaced logical reasoning as primary influences on the Court's decisions concerning this capital punishment issue.

The Rehnquist Court's *McCleskey* decision ignored racially discriminatory valuations of human life that were evident in capital sentencing. In *Payne*, the Court built upon that acceptance of discrimination by creating the opportunity for even broader discrimination through emotional decisions by jurors about which victims' lives should be avenged through the death penalty. After *Payne*, jurors are explicitly invited to focus on their subjective perceptions of the social worth of the victim rather than maintain the desired decision-making focus on the defendant's act and culpability. As a result of these decisions, discriminatory application of the death penalty by the race of the victim and defendant, and possibly by the social class of each as well, was enhanced by a Court that clearly indicated its disinclination to be vigilant in examining evidence of systemic discrimination in capital sentencing.

DEFINING ELIGIBILITY FOR EXECUTION

In several cases, the Rehnquist Court addressed the issue of eligibility for a death sentence. Under principles of criminal law, the age and mental capacity of defendants may affect whether they can be held responsible for crimes. Children, for example, may be regarded as too young to bear responsibility for criminal acts. The application of such traditional principles to the realm of capital punishment necessarily presents a line-drawing problem in which judges must develop a policy for determining if and when a defendant is too young or possesses some other limiting characteristics (e.g., mental retardation) that may constitutionally preclude a death sentence.

In *Thompson v. Oklahoma* (1988), the Court faced a challenge to a state statute which did not specify a minimum age of eligibility for capital punishment. As a fifteen year old, Thompson had participated in the brutal murder of a brother-in-law who had abused his sister. Thompson challenged his death sentence as violating the Eighth Amendment by claiming that the execution of someone for a crime committed as a teenager constituted cruel and unusual punishment. The case caused deep divisions within the Court. Of the eight justices who participated in the case, four found that the execution of anyone less than sixteen years of age at the time of the offense violated the contemporary standards of decency that define the Eighth Amendment. Justice O'Connor provided a fifth vote in favor of Thompson by concluding that a national consensus probably exists against the execution of fifteen-year-olds. By contrast, the three dissenters, Scalia, Rehnquist, and White, rejected the notion that there is a national consensus against such executions and argued that individualized decision making in capital cases can adequately account for consideration of each defendant's culpability and eligibility for a death sentence. The case left open the question of whether older teenagers could face execution.

The following year the Court clarified the issue by determining that defendants who commit capital crimes at the ages of sixteen and seventeen can be sentenced to death. In *Stanford v. Kentucky* (1989), newcomer Justice Kennedy joined the justices favoring eligibility for execution and O'Connor provided the needed fifth vote for drawing a clear line of eligibility between the ages of fifteen and sixteen. Justice Scalia's majority opinion relied heavily on the fact that many state statutes permit the execution of such teenaged offenders to provide evidence that contemporary societal standards do not preclude executions for these defendants. Because most death penalty states specifically permit youthfulness to be presented as a mitigating factor, he argued that the individualized decision making in each case could provide adequate consideration of the appropriateness of a death sentence for individual defendants. While the jurors may have the opportunity to differentiate between offenders, this application of discretion does not solve the fundamental problem involving violent youths' capacity to understand the nature and consequences of their actions. According to Victor Streib's (1989, 44) study of 34 juvenile death penalty cases,

> All but seven of these youths manifested a lack of understanding and concern about the death penalty both before committing their crimes and after being sentenced to death. For the younger and more [mentally] retarded ones, this may simply have stemmed from ignorance and immaturity. For the older ones, it may be illustrative of adolescents' endemic lack of understanding of the nature of death.

Despite these lingering issues, the Court's decision clarified constitutional standards with respect to the age of eligibility and thereby placed the United States out of step with many countries throughout the world which bar execution for acts committed prior to attainment of age eighteen.

The majority's disinterest in further exploring the issue of the appropriateness of capital punishment for youthful offenders was illustrated in *Johnson v. Texas* in 1993. At age nineteen, Johnson was convicted of killing a convenience store clerk during a robbery. The trial judge followed Texas law in instructing the jury to consider whether the killing was deliberate, whether there was a probability that the defendant would commit future violent acts, and any other mitigating and aggravating circumstances. After Johnson's conviction, the Texas law was invalidated by the Supreme Court in *Penry v. Lynaugh* (1989) because it did not adequately focus the jury's attention on Penry's mental retardation as a mitigating factor in considering whether to impose a death sentence. Johnson relied on *Penry* to challenge his death sentence by claiming that the trial procedures did not lead the jury to consider specifically the impact of his youthfulness on his culpability and the appropriateness of a death sentence. In a narrow 5-to-4 decision, the justices decided that the jury instruction inviting consideration of any mitigating circumstances adequately encompassed the issue of the defendant's age without any instruction to the jury to focus specifically on the teenager's youthfulness. Justice O'Connor, who had cast the decisive fifth vote to permit execution of teenage murderers, wrote the dissent. However, her defection did not alter the balance of power on the Court because Justice Clarence Thomas had replaced capital-punishment opponent Thurgood Marshall and Thomas consistently sided with the other conservative justices in supporting more flexible application of the death penalty.

As indicated in the reference to the *Penry* case, when confronted with the issue of mentally retarded defendants' eligibility for execution, the Court declined to place any clear limits on capital punishment. Such developmental disabilities were to be treated as mitigating factors. While the Burger Court had clearly stated that insane people could not be executed (*Ford v. Wainwright* 1985), the Rehnquist Court did not treat mental retardation as a bar to application of the death penalty. Although both situations raise questions about the putative deterrent and retributive value of execution for such persons, the Court again adopted the position that individualized decision making in capital cases could adequately take into consideration the appropriateness of the death penalty for each defendant. In the case of *Penry v. Lynaugh* (1989), concerning a defendant with the mental functioning of a seven-year-old, the Court approved the execution of mentally retarded persons but required that juries have the opportunity to take into consideration the mental capacity of the defendant before determining the sentence. Thus judges and juries retained the discretion to impose capital punishment on mentally retarded persons, including those who have little comprehension of the full implications of their actions.

The Rehnquist Court did not merely clarify eligibility for capital punishment through decisions affecting teenagers and the mentally retarded; they also enlarged the pool of eligible defendants by expanding juries' discretion in imposing the death penalty. The most significant such expansion affected felony-murder accomplices when the Court in 1987 revisited an issue that appeared to have been settled by a Burger Court decision in 1982.

In *Enmund v. Florida* (1982), two people attempted to rob an elderly couple at gunpoint at the couple's farmhouse. The couple resisted the robbery and managed to wound one of the robbers with a gunshot. The robbers responded by shooting and killing the elderly couple. Enmund was not one of the killers, but he was observed sitting in a car 200 yards from the farmhouse at the time of the shooting and was later seen driving the getaway car carrying the killers. Under Florida's felony-murder rule, Enmund was convicted for assisting in the crimes and sentenced to death. A sharply-divided Supreme Court decided that although Enmund could be convicted under the felony-murder rule, he could not be sentenced to death based upon his limited participation in the homicides. Such a penalty would be a disproportionate punishment in violation of the Eighth Amendment's prohibition on cruel and unusual punishments. For the majority, Justice White emphasized that Enmund could not be executed without evidence that he planned to kill or participated in the killing, and such evidence was particularly lacking in this case in which the killing seemed to result from resistance to the robbery rather than from a planned criminal homicide. According to White (*Enmund v. Florida* 1982, 801):

> For purposes of imposing the death penalty, Enmund's criminal culpability must be limited to his participation in the robbery, and his punishment must be tailored to his personal responsibility and moral guilt. Putting Enmund to death to avenge two killings that he did not commit and had no intention of committing or causing does not measurably contribute to the retributive end of ensuring that the criminal gets his just deserts.

The Court's decision was regarded as creating a bright-line rule that prevented criminal justice officials from seeking the death penalty unless defendants pulled the trigger or otherwise directly participated in the planning or execution of the homicide itself ("Recent Cases" 1983; Case Comment 1983). Justice O'Connor, joined by Justices Burger, Rehnquist, and Powell, wrote an extensive and highly critical dissent which completely disagreed with the majority's conclusions and argued that state criminal justice proceedings should be permitted to make their own determinations of defendants' culpability and appropriate punishment, including imposition of the death penalty for people convicted under felony-murder rules (*Enmund v. Florida* 1982, 802).

Five years later the issue returned to the now Rehnquist-led Supreme Court in the case of *Tison v. Arizona* (1987). The three Tison brothers, Donald, Ricky, and Raymond, assisted by other relatives, smuggled guns into a prison and helped their father, a convicted killer, and another prisoner escape. During their escape across a desert highway, their car had a flat tire. They flagged down a passing car occupied by the Lyons, a family of four, including an infant and fifteen-year-old girl. The Lyons family was taken to the Tisons' car which had been moved off the road and into the desert. The Tisons' father instructed his sons to go to the newly captured vehicle to obtain water. While getting the water, the brothers saw their father and the other escapee brutally murder the entire Lyons family. The Tison clan continued their escape in the Lyons' car but after a subsequent shoot-out at a police roadblock, Donald Tison was killed and the father died of exposure after escaping into the desert on foot. The remaining Tison brothers and other escapee were captured, convicted of murder, and sentenced to death. The Tison brothers challenged their death sentence under the bright-line rule that the Court had established in *Enmund* because they had not planned or directly participated in the killings (Alderman and Kennedy 1991).

The composition of the Court had not changed in a significant way during the intervening years. Justice Scalia had merely replaced another conservative, Chief Justice Burger. However, despite the lack of significant personnel changes, the Court decided that the Tisons could be executed for their felony-murder convictions. The opinion for the 5-4 majority was written by O'Connor. Although it was apparent from the vigorous dissent in *Enmund* that O'Connor and several of her colleagues in the *Tison* majority completely disagreed with the reasoning and result in *Enmund*, rather than overturn *Enmund*, the majority distinguished the *Tison* facts, obliterated the bright-line rule, and created a new amorphous standard permitting the death penalty in cases of "reckless indifference for human life" (*Tison v. Arizona* 1987, 158).

One analyst commented that it appeared puzzling that O'Connor bypassed an opportunity to overturn *Enmund* when she and her colleagues made it very clear that they disagreed with that decision ("Casenote" 1987). This commentator concluded that O'Connor created a new standard simply because the evidentiary record was better developed in *Tison* to establish the details of the felony-murder defendants' behavior (ibid., 375). However, the actual reason for O'Connor's strategy in substantially blurring the *Enmund* rule rather than abolishing it outright is not difficult to discern upon closer examination. O'Connor and the dissenters from *Enmund* needed to capture one vote from the *Enmund* majority in order to advance their policy preference for freer state discretion in the application of capital punishment. The addition of Scalia as a replacement for Burger simply maintained but did not expand the four-justice bloc that opposed *Enmund*. Thus the *Enmund* dissenters had to look to members of the *Enmund* majority to provide the decisive fifth vote to increase the applicability of capital punishment to accomplices. Among the members of the *Enmund* majority, Brennan and Marshall were clearly unavailable, because they continued to believe, as they had since *Furman*, that the death penalty always violates the Eighth Amendment. Justices Stevens and Blackmun were not likely candidates for defection because during that same term they expressed grave concerns about excessive discretion, discrimination, and arbitrary imposition of the death penalty in *McCleskey*. As it turned out, the only potential fifth vote available for capture was Justice White's. The prospect of persuading White to change sides was problematic, however, because he was, in fact, the author of the very *Enmund* opinion that O'Connor had vigorously denounced and that stood in the way of imposing the death penalty on the Tison brothers.

If O'Connor and her allies had sought to do what they obviously believed was the proper course of action, namely outright rejection of the bright-line rule against capital punishment for accomplices as established in *Enmund*, they would clearly not gain White's support unless he was willing to concede publicly that he had made a significant error in developing the rule in *Enmund*, the rule which he had authored. Thus O'Connor accommodated White's opinion in *Enmund* by purporting to distinguish it from *Tison* in order to capture White as the fifth vote to advance the conservatives' policy preference favoring more flexible application of capital punishment.

In this maneuvering, the *Enmund* rule was maintained, essentially in image rather than substance, in order to avoid placing White in the undesirable position of repudiating his own majority opinion from five years earlier, a position he may not have been willing to accept if the *Enmund* dissenters had pursued it. Thus the policy preferences of several justices were advanced through the creation of a vague rule which did not fit the actual views of either the *Enmund* dissenters, who wanted to give states freedom to execute felony-murder accomplices, or the four *Tison* dissenters, who did not think accomplices should receive death sentences. The new *Tison* standard and the resulting confusion in squaring it with the surviving rule from *Enmund* merely accommodated the fact that the Tisons' crime was horrible enough to move Justice White's preferred case outcome away from the clear rule which he had created in *Enmund*. The "Line of Death" for people convicted of murder, namely the permissible boundary for imposition of capital punishment, moved from the relatively clear *Enmund* rule requiring direct participation in a killing in order to permit executions to the broader, vaguer "reckless indifference" rule, which necessarily involves greater discretion by prosecutors, juries, and judges as well as increased opportunities for discriminatory outcomes.

The Rehnquist Court effectively terminated the prohibition on capital punishment for accomplices and created a rule which permits judges and juries to impose the death penalty on nearly any murder accomplice. If the decision makers find the accomplice sufficiently unsavory or the murder sufficiently horrible, they can impose a death sentence merely by labeling the defendant's action as "reckless disregard for human life," without concerning themselves with whether or not this defendant's participation and culpability was actually greater than those of other defendants who do not receive the death penalty. The *Tison* rule represented a very significant expansion of discretionary decision making with attendant consequences for broadening the pool of defendants eligible for execution and discriminating in an inconsistent fashion between those chosen to live and those slated to die.

GUIDING DECISION MAKING BY JURIES

In *Woodson* (1976), the Burger Court had barred the automatic imposition of the death penalty because such mandatory sentences precluded the opportunity for individualized consideration of sentences under the principles of *Gregg* (1976). Initially, the Rehnquist Court upheld this principle by invalidating a statute that mandated a death sentence for people convicted of murder while already serving a sentence of life without parole (*Sumner v. Schuman* 1987). Subsequently, however, the Court permitted state legislatures to direct juries' decision making through the imposition of mandatory sentences in some circumstances. In *Blystone v. Pennsylvania* (1990), the defendant robbed and murdered a hitchhiker and subsequently bragged to friends about how much he enjoyed killing his victim. The jury found the existence of an aggravating factor, commission of a killing while in the perpetration of a felony, but the jury did not find the existence of any mitigating factors. Under Pennsylvania law, the jury was required to impose the death penalty if it unanimously found the existence of at least one specified aggravating factor without finding any mitigating factors. Despite the inherent clash between this mandatory death penalty and true individualized consideration which would give the jury an option of imposing life imprisonment, a five-member majority upheld the Pennsylvania law. The majority concluded that consideration of aggravating and mitigating factors provided sufficient individualized decision making in spite of the imposition of the mandatory sentence. The nature of the *Blystone* decision raised the possibility that the Rehnquist Court favored increased discretion for jury decision making when such discretion could be applied, as in *Tison*, to impose capital punishment on a wider range of defendants. However, when increased discretion might lead a jury to decline to impose capital punishment, then the Court indicated that it could accept a mandatory sentencing scheme for imposition of the death penalty.

The Rehnquist Court's actions affecting capital punishment have not represented a direct dismantling of the Burger Court's framework for decision making concerning death sentences. In *Blystone*, for example, the Court maintained the existing requirement of consideration of aggravating and mitigating factors but merely ensured that death sentences would be imposed in certain cases by endorsing a state legislature's prohibition on truly individualized decision making in certain categories of cases. In other cases, the justices also maintained the Burger Court doctrines that endeavored to avoid capricious imposition of capital punishment. In *Dawson v. Delaware* (1992), for example, the entire Court except for Justice Thomas barred from use as evidence information about a murderer's membership in a racist organization when there was no hint of racism in the killing of a same-race victim by a prison escapee. Such information could inflame the jury and clash with the defendant's First Amendment right of association without having any relevance to the defendant's culpability. The Court also prevented trial judges from barring consideration of certain mitigating factors (*Hitchcock v. Dugger* 1987) and declared unconstitutionally vague an aggravating circumstances statute that referred to "especially heinous, atrocious, or cruel" murders (*Maynard v. Cartwright* 1988). In *Simmons v. South Carolina* (1994), the Court found a due process violation when the trial judge refused to inform the jury that the defendant would be ineligible for parole if given a life sentence instead of the death penalty. Thus the Rehnquist Court has made several decisions that seek to ensure that juries have access to adequate and relevant information before deciding the defendant's fate in capital cases.

On the other hand, the Rehnquist Court justices were also clearly willing to give judges and juries greater flexibility and discretion for imposing capital punishment, especially as the era progressed and the stalwart death penalty opponents, Brennan and Marshall, retired and were replaced by more conservative justices. For example, in *Walton v. Arizona* (1990), a narrow five-member majority approved Arizona's practice of requiring the judge rather than the jury to make findings about the existence of aggravating and mitigating factors. This conclusion dismayed Justice Stevens, in particular, who believed that the Sixth Amendment right to trial by jury requires that a jury determine the facts before a death sentence can be imposed. The Arizona statute approved by the Court also placed a burden on the defense for showing the nature and sufficiency of mitigating evidence, a requirement that necessarily limited the fact-finder's ability to make findings favorable to the defendant. In *Arave v. Creech* (1993), the Court approved Idaho's "utter disregard for human life" aggravating circumstance over the objections of Justices Stevens and Blackmun, who believed that the provision was unconstitutionally vague and did not adequately guide the jury's consideration of the factors relevant to a possible sentence of death.

In *Romano v. Oklahoma* (1994), a five-member majority saw no problem with the presentation to the jury of evidence concerning the defendant's death sentence in a separate case. The four dissenters felt strongly that there was a grave risk that the jurors would freely, if not automatically, sentence the defendant to death because their knowledge about the other death sentence would relieve them of a sense of responsibility for making a careful, considered judgment about the life or death decision. Was the other death sentence relevant to the jury's decision? The jury might be told that the defendant was convicted of another murder, as this might bear on an aggravating factor concerning the probability of future violence by the defendant. However, the jury's knowledge of the defendant's sentence for that crime would seem likely either to inflame the jury's passions against the defendant or to make the jury feel less responsible for making a careful life or death decision. Once again, the Court's decision constituted a subtle expansion of flexibility and opportunity for broader imposition of the death penalty.

THE EMERGING VISIONS OF JUSTICES SCALIA AND THOMAS

As in the non-capital Eighth Amendment cases, Justices Scalia and Thomas have asserted themselves in capital punishment cases in an effort to give states greater flexibility in imposing death sentences. Although their views have not prevailed (yet), they are among the youngest justices on the Supreme Court, and therefore their tenures may outlast those of the colleagues with whom they disagree. Moreover, through their assertive opinions, they are laying the groundwork for any future justices who share their jurisprudential vision to carry forward the arguments and reasoning developed in contemporary cases (Smith 1995a).

Consistent with their view that federal courts should defer to the policies and judgments of state governmental officials, Scalia and Thomas have generally opposed judicial scrutiny of and interference with the imposition of the death penalty. In a careful study of Scalia's decisions on capital punishment, one scholar concluded that "Scalia seems to believe that there are virtually no constitutional limits on a state's imposition of the death penalty" (Gey 1992, 102).

Scalia's initial written opinion concerning the death penalty was a unanimous majority opinion reversing and remanding for reconsideration a death sentence imposed without consideration of nonstatutory mitigating factors (*Hitchcock v. Dugger* 1987). This was by no means an indication that Scalia had doubts about the propriety of how the death penalty was generally applied. The case that gave rise to his initial opinion merely failed to tap Scalia's growing concerns about judicial interference with states' imposition of the death penalty. Scalia's support for capital punishment was clear in other decisions during his first term. Most notably, he was among the five justices in the majority who refused to consider powerful statistical evidence of systemic racial discrimination in Georgia's death sentences as an indication of constitutional infirmity in the *McCleskey* case during the same year. And, as indicated in the foregoing discussion, Scalia's memorandum to his colleagues in the *McCleskey* case demonstrated that he recognized the existence of racial discrimination in Georgia's system and accepted that the statistics demonstrated the pervasiveness of discrimination, yet he provided the decisive vote to preserve the death penalty in spite of this equal protection problem.

In his first term as a justice, Scalia began to criticize the Court's decisions that controlled what information could be considered by judges and juries in deciding whether or not to impose the death penalty. In *Booth*, when the Court decided in 1987 that victim impact statements were impermissible in the sentencing phase of capital cases because they may improperly lead to arbitrary and capricious imposition of the death penalty, Scalia spoke on behalf of the four dissenters. Scalia implied that capital sentencing procedures that permit the introduction of mitigating factors show favoritism to defendants and reiterated his familiar theme that policy decisions, including those affecting capital punishment, should be decided by branches of government other than the judiciary (*Booth v. Maryland* 1987, 520):

> Many citizens have found one-sided and hence unjust the criminal trial in which a parade of witnesses comes forth to testify to the pressures beyond normal human experience that drove the defendant to commit his crime, with no one to lay before the sentencing authority the full reality of human suffering the defendant has produced -- which (and *not* moral guilt alone) is one of the reasons society deems his act worthy of the prescribed penalty. Perhaps these sentiments do not sufficiently temper justice with mercy, but that is a question to be decided through the democratic processes of a free people, and not by the decrees of this Court. There is nothing in the Constitution that dictates the answer, no more in the field of capital punishment than elsewhere.

Scalia's advocacy of shifting the sentencers' emphasis from moral guilt to subjective perceptions of the degree of harm--the view that subsequently prevailed in *Payne*--raised risks that discriminatory application of the death penalty would result when some victims' lives were considered by jurors to have been more valuable than other victims' lives. With respect to Scalia's desire to diminish judicial interference in states' capital punishment practices, his willingness to defer the definition of policies potentially affecting individuals' rights to decisions by elected officials is a component of his consistent theme emphasizing "popular control of public policy through representative institutions and respect for the majority's policy choices" (Brisbin 1990, 5). Such a policy can leave political minorities disadvantaged, or even unprotected, as demonstrated by the abdication of judicial responsibility for equal protection of law in the *McCleskey* case and its attendant discriminatory consequences for African-American capital defendants and victims.

Scalia's desire to end judicial limitations on the factors that sentencers can consider in deciding whether or not to impose the death penalty was presented most forcefully in a concurring opinion in *Walton v. Arizona* (1990). Scalia argued that there was an inherent conflict between the Court's effort in *Furman v. Georgia* (1972) to channel sentencers' discretion and later cases that required sentencers to consider mitigating evidence rather than imposing mandatory sentences (*Woodson v. North Carolina*) and that prevented states from limiting the kinds of mitigating circumstances that could be considered (*Lockett v. Ohio*). According to Scalia, "[T]he practice which in *Furman* had been described as the discretion to sentence to death and pronounced constitutionally prohibited, was in *Woodson* and *Lockett* renamed the discretion not to sentence to death and pronounced constitutionally required" (*Walton v. Arizona* 1990, 662). Scalia even applied his characteristic biting sarcasm to ridicule the two doctrines that he viewed as in conflict (ibid., 664):

> To acknowledge that "there perhaps is an inherent tension between this line of cases and the line stemming from *Furman*"...is rather like saying that there was perhaps an inherent tension between the Allies and the Axis Powers in World War II. And to refer to the two lines as pursuing "twin objectives" ...is rather like referring to the twin objectives of good and evil. They cannot be reconciled.

Scalia also took the opportunity to enunciate a narrow view of the Eighth Amendment which, consistent with his other opinions, provided little basis for judges to identify violations (ibid., 670):

> When punishments other than fines are involved, the Amendment explicitly requires a court to consider not only whether the penalty is severe or harsh, but also whether it is "unusual." If it is not, then the Eighth Amendment does not prohibit it, no matter how cruel a judge might think it to be. Moreover, the Eighth Amendment's prohibition is directed against cruel and unusual *punishments*. It does not, by its terms, regulate the procedures of sentencing as opposed to the substance of punishment....Thus, the procedural elements of a sentencing scheme come within the prohibition, if at all, only when they are of such a

nature as systematically to render the infliction of
cruel punishment "unusual."

Scalia went on to say that a mandatory death sentence for crimes
traditionally punished by death "cannot possibly violate the Eighth
Amendment, because it will not be 'cruel' (neither absolutely nor for
a particular crime) and it will not be 'unusual' (neither in the sense
of being a type of penalty that is not traditional nor in the sense of
being rarely or 'freakishly' imposed)" (ibid., 671). Because, in
Scalia's view, the "*Woodson-Lockett* line of cases...bears no relation
whatever to the text of the Eighth Amendment" (ibid.), he rejected any
claim that they might deserve protection under *stare decisis*. In other
cases, Scalia continued his attacks on judicial requirements and limits
(i.e., the "channeling" of mitigating discretion) on the factors
considered by judges and juries in sentencing (*McKoy v. North
Carolina* 1990; *Sochor v. Florida* 1992; *Johnson v. Texas* 1993).

A footnote in Justice Blackmun's *Walton* dissent accused Justice
Scalia of threatening "the integrity of this Court's adjudicative process"
by attacking settled Eighth Amendment doctrines that were not briefed
and argued in the case (*Walton v. Arizona* 1990, 680). According to
Blackmun, "It is disturbing that the decisive vote in a capital case
should turn on a single Justice's rejection of a line of authority that
both parties to this controversy, and eight Members of this Court, have
accepted" (ibid.).

In the Court's 1989 decision that implicitly determined that the
Constitution did not preclude the execution of mentally retarded persons
convicted of murder (*Penry v. Lynaugh* 1989), Scalia's opinion
emphasized that such executions violate neither the original intent of the
Eighth Amendment nor evolving standards of decency (ibid., 351). He
also pressed his theme that the Court should not require juries to
consider mitigating factors (ibid., 360).

Near the end of his career, Justice Blackmun concluded that the
death penalty is always unconstitutional and for a brief period prior to
his retirement undertook to protest, as Brennan and Marshall had done
before him, by dissenting in capital cases. This new position was
announced in a dissenting opinion in *Callins v. Collins* (1994), a case
denying a petition for a writ of certiorari from a death-row inmate
scheduled for imminent execution. According to Blackmun, capital
punishment is inevitably and hopelessly flawed: "The problem is that
the inevitability of factual, legal, and moral error gives us a system that
we know must wrongly kill some defendants, a system that fails to
deliver the fair, consistent, and reliable sentences of death required by
the Constitution" (*Callins v. Collins* 1994, 1130). Dissents from

denials of writs of certiorari are unusual but regular occurrences when individual justices feel very strongly about an issue. The extraordinary aspect of the *Callins* case was that Scalia wrote a concurring opinion simply to highlight and attack Blackmun's difficult conclusion generated by twenty years of personal struggle with death penalty cases. Consistent with his strident style (Smith 1993c), Scalia seized the opportunity to strongly repudiate the basis for Blackmun's conclusion. In Scalia's view (*Callins v. Collins* 1994, 1128),

> If the people conclude that...more brutal murders may be deterred by capital punishment; indeed, if they merely conclude that justice requires such brutal deaths to be avenged by capital punishment; the creation of false, untextual and unhistorical contradictions with "the Court's Eighth Amendment jurisprudence" should not prevent them.

Scalia not only has fought for a significant reduction, if not elimination, of judicial constraints upon states' freedom to apply capital punishment, he has shown dogged determination in seizing available opportunities to refute his philosophical opponents and advance his views.

When Justice Thomas arrived at the Supreme Court, his opinions in death penalty cases directly echoed many of Scalia's themes. Like Scalia, Thomas objected to what he saw as a tension between the Court's overriding goal in *Furman* of preventing capricious death penalty decisions and the Court's requirement, especially in *Penry*, that juries consider mitigating evidence (*Graham v. Collins* 1993, 479). Thomas took Scalia's objection a step further by asserting that the consideration of mitigating factors and the abolition of mandatory death penalties contribute to racial discrimination. According to Thomas, "To withhold the death penalty out of sympathy for a defendant who is a member of a favored group is not different from a decision to impose the penalty on the basis of a negative bias" (ibid., 495). Thomas thus indicated that a return to a mandatory death penalty would eliminate racial discrimination in capital sentencing. In Thomas's words, "One would think, however, that by eliminating explicit jury discretion and treating all defendants equally, a mandatory death penalty scheme was a perfectly reasonable legislative response to the concerns [about arbitrariness and discrimination] expressed in *Furman*" (ibid., 487). Thomas also reiterated Scalia's theme of using majoritarian preferences manifested by elected officials to guide policy decisions affecting capital punishment: "I believe this Court should leave it to elected state legislators, 'representing organized society,' to decide which factors are 'particularly relevant to the sentencing decision'" (ibid., 499).

The return to mandatory death sentences espoused by Scalia and Thomas has some intuitive appeal as a means to eliminate the complications of aggravating and mitigating factors and, in Thomas's mind, as a means to reduce discrimination through standardization. In reality, however, mandatory sentences would do nothing to eliminate arbitrary and discriminatory application of capital punishment. In essence, the mandatory sentences envisioned by Scalia and Thomas would fail by misapprehending the nature of discretionary decision making that underlies determinations about the death penalty and infuses judgments throughout the criminal justice system. A mandatory sentencing scheme focuses only on a single decision point: the imposition of sentence. Therefore, it does not eliminate the application of discretion in the cumulative decisions that shape the ultimate sentencing outcomes. A death sentence is the product of a number of identifiable decisions, including: the prosecutor's decision to seek the death penalty against a specific defendant; the prosecutor's decision to engage in plea bargaining; the trial strategies and arguments put forward by prosecutors and defense attorneys; the trial judge's rulings on evidence and motions; judges' and lawyers' decisions during the selection of jurors; a convicted defendant's decision about whether or not to express remorse during the sentencing hearing; and judges' and jurors' determinations about the existence (or lack thereof) of aggravating and mitigating factors (White 1991). According to Welsh White (1991, 137), "[M]ost knowledgeable observers agree that the switch to the post-*Furman* statutes has had only a minimal effect on racial discrimination in capital sentencing. Perhaps the most significant reason for this is that racial prejudice is a powerful force that may not be easily extirpated by statutory or verbal formulas." Unconscious biases about the worth of the victim or the dangerousness of the defendant can seep into the decision-making processes at any point and affect the final outcome. For a example, a prosecutor may, without even realizing it, react more strongly against the murder of a prominent local citizen than against the killing of an unskilled laborer. Visceral reactions may be affected by the prosecutor's unconscious empathy for or aversion to victims and defendants according to their racial (or social class or age or gender) classifications. The same may be true of conscious or unconscious biases affecting the decisions of judges and jurors. Thus mandatory sentences and other adjustments in the sentencing process cannot eliminate unequal results in a process comprised of cumulative discretionary decisions by multiple decision makers.

Although capital cases involve extra procedural steps, such as bifurcated proceedings, which are presumed to increase the reliability and fairness of decisions, Samuel Gross (1996) has demonstrated that capital cases are actually especially susceptible to erroneous decisions, in part because of the discretion employed by justice system officials. For example, in homicide cases, police may feel public pressure to "close" the case with an arrest, even in evidentiary circumstances in which the police would leave lesser crimes "open" for further investigation. This pressure may also spur officers to engage in especially manipulative techniques during interrogation which may produce incriminating statements, even by innocent suspects. Prosecutors' desire to reassure the public with an arrest and conviction in a homicide case may make them more susceptible to plea bargain agreements with suspects who volunteer to "finger" a killer, even though the witness may, in fact, be the real killer. This may be especially true when there are no other surviving witnesses to contradict the cooperative suspect's version of events. Prosecutors are also less likely to drop cases when they personally doubt the evidence. As is not the case with lesser offenses, public pressure may lead the prosecutor to let the jury decide--thus making murder suspects more likely to face the chancy ordeal of trial in which jurors' preconceptions and prejudices may have a significant impact. Moreover, the publicity attendant to a murder trial and the exclusion of potential jurors who are strongly opposed to the death penalty increase the likelihood of conviction in capital cases. Unbeknownst to Scalia, Thomas, and the other justices, all of these factors serve to increase the risks of discriminatory and erroneous decisions in death penalty cases.

The opinions of Scalia and Thomas are laying a groundwork for significant reductions in judicial supervision of capital punishment. The ultimate results of their efforts will be determined by future changes in the composition of the Supreme Court--changes which may occur in the near future or may not occur for several decades. In any event, current and future justices are confronted with a series of strongly presented arguments favoring judicial deference to the capital punishment policies developed and implemented by the individual states.

CONCLUSION

The fundamental decision about whether the United States would, by judicial decree, abolish capital punishment was made in *Gregg* during the Burger Court era. However, the Rehnquist Court has had a significant impact on how and against whom the death penalty will be imposed. The Burger Court's *Gregg* decision presumed that clearer guidelines for decision makers, such as bifurcated proceedings and the consideration of mitigating and aggravating circumstances, would eliminate the problems of arbitrariness and discrimination. Subsequently, the Rehnquist Court was presented with powerful evidence about the persistence of such problems, yet the philosophical orientations and policy preferences of the majority of justices led them to protect capital punishment against social science-based challenges. Moreover, the Rehnquist Court's decisions have clarified and broadened the applicability of capital punishment by endorsing the death penalty as a punishment for teenagers, the mentally retarded, and felony-murder accomplices. Although the Court has not gone as far as Scalia and Thomas would like in freeing the states to apply capital punishment without judicial interference, the Rehnquist Court's decisions have had the overall impact of making it easier for states to impose the death penalty. Several of the Court's decisions have sought to preserve the *Gregg* framework for channeling decision making, but the Court's acceptance of vague aggravating factors makes clear that there is no intention to provide stricter controls on capital punishment. Moreover, just as Justices Scalia and Thomas became assertive spokespersons in favor of relaxed judicial standards, the retirements of Justices Brennan, Marshall, and Blackmun removed the countervailing voices that sought to move the United States into line with the other Western democracies that have abolished capital punishment as a barbaric relic of the past. Because the Rehnquist Court's new Democratic appointees, Justices Ruth Bader Ginsburg and Stephen Breyer, are more moderate than their liberal predecessors (*e.g., Tuilaepa v. California* 1994), the Supreme Court is less frequently a forum for debate between opposing sides. Instead, the Court's decisions and the reasoning contained in the Court's opinions have moved firmly and steadily in favor of endorsing broader and more flexible applications of the death penalty.

CHAPTER 4

Access to Justice
on the Road to Punishment

The Supreme Court's impact on criminal punishment is not limited to Eighth Amendment decisions that evaluate the permissibility of particular sanctions. The Supreme Court also affects the fates of convicted offenders through decisions that define the nature of judicial processes. These judicial decisions determine such issues as the scope and nature of the right to counsel and offenders' access to appellate reviews of their convictions. It is with respect to these judicial process issues that the Rehnquist Court may have had its most profound impact upon criminal punishment.

THE RIGHT TO COUNSEL

In theory, the American justice process is based on an adversarial model in which the truth about guilt and innocence will emerge from the courtroom clash between prosecutors and defense attorneys. In the 1960s, the Supreme Court sought to give broad application to this theory by interpreting the Sixth Amendment right to counsel to require the appointment of defense attorneys for all defendants facing serious charges (*Gideon v. Wainwright* 1963) and for all first appeals of right in state criminal cases (*Douglas v. California* 1963). Later the Burger Court era justices expanded the right to counsel at the trial level to cover all cases in which the defendant faced incarceration (*Argersinger v. Hamlin* 1972), but they denied the existence of any such right when the defendant faced only a fine (*Scott v. Illinois* 1979) and in discretionary appeals (*Ross v. Moffitt* 1974). Other Warren-era cases, which also implicated the Fifth Amendment privilege against compelled self-incrimination, defined when defendants were entitled to have counsel present, such as during questioning by police after arrest

(*Miranda v. Arizona* 1966) and during post-indictment line-ups (*United States v. Wade* 1967).

Although these decisions established the "if" and "when" of the right to counsel, they did not define standards for competence and effectiveness of counsel in representing defendants. Because criminal defendants face serious deprivations of their liberty and, in some cases, even their lives, it would seem important to insure that the attorneys representing defendants meet specified standards for professional performance. However, the Supreme Court during the Burger era indicated its reluctance to step too deeply into the difficult issue of defining minimal performance standards for the effectuation of a substantive right to counsel. In two important cases (*Strickland v. Washington* 1984; *United States v. Cronic* 1984), the Burger-era justices established vague, minimal standards for attorneys' performance that made it nearly impossible for defendants to establish that their attorneys' actions had been so inadequate as to produce constitutionally deficient ineffective assistance of counsel. The justices are loath to place judges in the position of second-guessing lawyers' strategies and performances and therefore questions about minimum competence focus on whether the attorney met reasonable professional standards and whether a deficient performance had a demonstrable impact on the case's outcome. Critics of the Court's standards have joked about them as equaling a "mirror test": you put a mirror under the court-appointed attorney's nose, and if the mirror clouds up to demonstrate that he or she is breathing, that's adequate counsel (Bright, Kinnard, and Webster 1990)

Does the right to counsel amount to more than simply a right to have someone with a law degree standing at your side when you are processed, convicted, and sentenced? Obviously, no one would answer "yes" to this statement as a matter of constitutional ideals, yet many cases appear to prove the accuracy of this characterization. For example, the attorney for a woman facing a death sentence for murdering her abusive husband in Alabama not only failed to obtain hospital records to show the injuries that his client suffered from her husband's abuse (Lacayo 1992), he was also so drunk during the trial that he was found in contempt of court and held in jail overnight until he was sober enough to continue the trial the next day (Bright 1994). Not surprisingly, the defendant was convicted and sentenced to death. A court-appointed attorney for capital defendants in Texas became well-known for how quickly he moved his client's cases along through trial, not for his success in representing defendants. He bragged that he spent little time doing legal research or even taking notes (Barrett

1994). In other examples, lawyers in death penalty cases never read their state's capital punishment statute, failed to cite any cases in appellate briefs, and failed to talk to their clients before filing appeals (Gershman 1993).

Because attorneys appointed to represent indigent defendants are often assigned to cases by elected judges, there are risks that appointments will be based on political patronage rather than experience and expertise. For example, Cleveland, Ohio has public defenders, salaried attorneys who handle criminal defense for poor defendants on a full-time basis. However, the local judges bypass the public defenders for death-penalty murder cases and award these cases with their $12,500 state-paid fees to private attorneys who may not necessarily have significant interest and experience in such legal matters (Torassa 1993). In other locales, defendants are hampered by a lack of resources that may deter experienced attorneys from accepting cases and prevent inexperienced attorneys from providing effective assistance. Alabama, for example, paid appointed defense counsel in capital cases just $20 per hour with a $1,000 maximum for out-of-court investigation and case preparation (Coyle 1990). Counsel for indigent defendants also lack funds for hiring investigators, psychiatrists, and expert witnesses, resources that are usually available to their fully-funded adversaries in the prosecutor's office. Some judges have reportedly appointed inexperienced or unproven attorneys to capital cases with the apparent intention of reducing the risk that they might preside over the acquittal of a defendant in a controversial murder case (Bowers 1983).

Does adequately funded, thorough representation make a difference with respect to who receives criminal punishment, including the death penalty? No one disputes that resources and professional expertise can have a significant impact on case outcomes. When retired football star, broadcaster, and actor, O.J. Simpson, stood trial in 1995 for murdering his wife and a waiter who was returning the sunglasses she had left at a restaurant, the most outstanding feature of the murder trial was not simply its nationally televised notoriety but its clear demonstration that significant resources and expertise can position a defendant well to challenge the weaknesses in a prosecutor's case (Gleick 1995). Simpson was able to afford representation from several of the nation's most prominent defense attorneys as well as assistance from nationally known forensic experts. These resources made pivotal contributions to his acquittal.

Abundant evidence illustrates the disadvantages experienced by criminal defendants who are represented by burned-out public defenders (*e.g.*, Smolowe 1993; Applebome 1992) or inexperienced appointed counsel (*e.g.*, Coyle 1990). In addition, there are individual examples, such as Federico Martinez Macias who spent nearly 10 years on death row. He was convicted of capital murder in Texas at a trial in which his court-appointed attorney, who was paid only $11.84 per hour, spent only $500 on investigation and expert witnesses and failed to present testimony from an alibi witness who placed Macias miles from the crime scene at the time of the murder. Macias was convicted based on the testimony of an admitted participant in the robbery-murder who was permitted to plead guilty to lesser charges in exchange for his agreement to identify the "real" killer. When a prominent Washington, D.C., law firm eventually volunteered to handle the post-conviction defense proceedings, Macias gained his freedom after his new lawyers devoted significant resources and expertise to investigating the case thoroughly and presenting new evidence to an appellate court (Cohen 1955).

Because American society must make policy choices about the allocation and expenditure of resources, it is not feasible to expect that all defendants can receive equal representation in a scarce-resource environment. Money must be spent on a variety of public programs and the defense of indigent criminal defendants will never receive ideal levels of funding. Although the Supreme Court does not design and manage indigent defense systems created by states and counties for providing representation for criminal defendants, the Court does set the standards which guide such systems by determining the permissibility of practices and performance. A recognition that representation can never be equal does not mean that representation cannot be pushed toward greater adequacy through stricter supervision by federal judges at the behest of the Supreme Court. The stigma and deprivation of liberty (or life) attendant to a criminal conviction have such a significant impact on people's lives that there is strong reason to give greater substance to the constitutional ideal of right to counsel that underlies the American adversarial justice system. However, despite their role (or potential role) in pushing local governments to make the right to counsel a substantive reality rather than a symbolic entitlement, the decisions of the Rehnquist Court have reinforced minimal standards for defense counsel and further reduced the likelihood that the imposition of criminal punishment will be produced by careful and fair decisions.

In a capital case in 1987, the Rehnquist Court rejected a claim that an attorney demonstrated ineffective assistance of counsel by failing to present mitigating evidence during the sentencing hearing prior to imposition of the death penalty (*Burger v. Kemp* 1987). In a later case, the justices further relaxed the already-difficult-to-establish standards for ineffective assistance of counsel in rejecting a defendant's claim in a case in which he would have received life in prison instead of a death sentence if his attorney had raised an appropriate objection to an improperly presented aggravating factor (*Lockhart v. Fretwell* 1993). Such decisions move further away from the development of professional standards which will ensure that defendants receive competent representation before being deprived of liberty or their lives through criminal punishment.

Although issues of attorney resources and competence fall most heavily upon indigent defendants, the Rehnquist Court acted to place even more defendants into the indigent category where they would receive counsel assigned by the state rather than choose their own attorneys. In a pair of cases in 1989 (*United States v. Monsanto* 1989; *Caplin & Drysdale v. United States* 1989), the Court ruled that government forfeiture rules concerning proceeds from narcotics trafficking could be used to prevent defendants from hiring attorneys of their own choosing. Under such rules, the government can seize defendants' assets before the defendants have been convicted of any crime. According to one scholar, the Rehnquist Court "succeeded not only in undermining the essence of the adversary system but it also gave the government virtually unfettered discretion to deter and disqualify talented or aggressive defense counsel from representing defendants in complex drug-related cases" (Garcia 1992, 37). Other scholars have echoed this concern about the adverse effect on non-indigent defendants' traditional right to retain counsel of choice in order to have confidence in the adequacy and competence of representation (Decker 1992).

Because the United States has appellate courts, there are presumably opportunities for judges to catch and correct any errors made by trial judges and underpaid or inexperienced defense attorneys. However, there is no constitutional right to counsel for indigent convicted offenders beyond the first appeal of right which is normally presented to a state's intermediate appellate court. For discretionary appeals to a state supreme court or collateral habeas corpus actions seeking review by the federal courts, the prisoner must represent him- or herself if there is no money to hire private counsel. A patchwork system of state-funded or privately funded legal assistance programs may provide representation or assistance in some instances. However, the existence and size of such programs are dependent on the resource allocation decisions and voluntarism of external actors. Even in death penalty cases, there is no constitutional right to legal representation for post-conviction processes after the initial appeal. The Rehnquist Court made this point quite clear in a 1989 decision (*Murray v. Giarratano*), despite complaints from Justice Stevens about the high rate of procedural and other errors discovered in capital cases when attorneys are available to provide professional representation for convicted offenders (Greenhouse 1989b). Thus the Rehnquist Court's limited interpretation of the Sixth Amendment and lack of concern about the flaws in trial representation of indigent defendants left even prisoners facing execution with few options for challenging purported errors in their trials. Although a few prisoners have become adept at representing themselves as self-educated jailhouse lawyers (Kaplan and Cohn 1991), the vast majority of prisoners have little hope of representing themselves due to lack of education, deficient access to legal materials, illiteracy, mental illness, and other impediments to self-education in the arcane details of law (Smith 1987). For many of those prisoners who must represent themselves, the task of legal research and case preparation became even more difficult as a result of the Court's 1996 decision in *Lewis v. Casey*. This decision required them to show "injury-in-fact" before a judge could find a violation of their right of access to the courts and thereby order the provision of additional library resources or legal assistance. As noted in chapter 2, this requirement can place prisoners in a "catch-22" situation of requiring knowledge of law and legal procedures in order to prove that they need assistance in order to make use of law and legal procedures. Unlike the cases of prisoners convicted and incarcerated for committing lesser crimes, there are organized efforts to find lawyers to handle post-conviction processes in death penalty cases on a voluntary basis. However, there is a serious shortage of attorneys willing to donate the substantial time and money needed to handle such cases effectively (Smothers 1993).

Congress has sought to address this problem for death penalty cases by providing a statutory right to counsel for capital cases' post-conviction proceedings in the federal courts. The Rehnquist Court, however, came within a single vote of consigning this statutory initiative to the realm of hollow symbolism. As this chapter will shortly describe in greater detail, the Court undertook judicially initiated reform of habeas corpus procedures by, among other things, requiring that convicted offenders seeking review of state court convictions file only a single petition containing all of their claims (*McCleskey v. Zant* 1991). Subsequent petitions from the same prisoners can be dismissed for violating the prohibition on successive petitions even if they raise new, credible issues. A Texas prisoner came within hours of his execution without ever securing representation from an attorney for his federal habeas corpus claim. He requested an attorney in accordance with the purpose of the statute, but Texas sought to proceed with his execution anyway on the claim that he had violated the statute's procedures. Texas claimed that he could not simply request an attorney. Instead, the state argued that an attorney could not be appointed until the prisoner filed a habeas corpus petition on his own. The prisoner asserted, however, that he needed the attorney first in order to prepare a proper habeas petition. Since he is only entitled to one petition, it would do him little good to have an attorney help him *after* he had already filed and become bound by the claims amateurishly stated in a homemade petition (Labaton 1994). By the slimmest of margins, a five-member majority of the Court decided that the execution could be halted until an attorney was provided in accordance with the federal statute (*McFarland v. Scott* 1994). Four justices believed that federal court judges should not possess so much power over the decision about whether or not an execution can be delayed. In effect, they would permit executions to go forward while prisoners are still seeking fulfillment of the statutory right to be represented by an attorney in federal habeas proceedings.

The Rehnquist Court has made it easier for states to impose criminal punishment by declining to use their interpretive powers to give strengthened substantive meaning to the Sixth Amendment right to counsel. By relaxing standards for attorney competence and impeding fulfillment of the adversary ideal, the justices have shortened the path from prosecution to punishment. As documented by John Decker (1992), the Court's decisions that reduce Fourth Amendment protections against unreasonable searches and seizures and that limit Fifth Amendment rights also have the effect of easing the tasks of police and prosecutors in gaining convictions. However, the Sixth Amendment decisions provide especially telling evidence of the Court's direction because of the presumed importance of the right to counsel and the relative clarity of landmark decisions establishing the contours of the right.

HABEAS CORPUS REFORM

Habeas corpus petitions provide the vehicle through which criminal offenders convicted in state courts seek federal judicial review of their convictions. If prisoners believe their federal constitutional rights were violated in the course of the state court prosecutions that produced their convictions, they may petition federal judges to review the actions of state criminal justice officials.

The American legal system inherited the Writ of Habeas Corpus, frequently known as the "Great Writ," from England. It provides the basis for anyone detained by the government, including those in mental institutions, to challenge the basis for their detention. The importance of habeas corpus is underscored by the fact that it is one of the few individual rights protected in the original Constitution. Two years before the framers of the Constitution placed individual rights and liberties in the Constitution through the Bill of Rights, they had stated in Article I, Section 9 that "[t]he Privilege of the Writ of Habeas Corpus shall not be suspended, unless when in Cases of Rebellion or Invasion the public Safety may require it."

Although Congress cannot suspend habeas corpus except in extraordinary national emergencies, Congress can enact statutes to shape the application of and procedures for habeas corpus petitions. Congress began to use its authority to define habeas corpus procedures through the Habeas Corpus Act of 1867, and it has continued to govern habeas procedures through subsequent legislative enactments (28 U.S.C. sec. 2254). While some critics would like to bar state prisoners' cases from the federal courts, Congress has clearly endorsed the role of federal courts in reviewing state convictions through the vehicle of habeas corpus. As Larry Yackle (1994, 702) observed, "recent [congressional] enactments, particularly the establishment of the federal rules for habeas practice in 1977, close the books on the question whether current law makes the federal forum available to state prisoners."

Since 1968, critics have regularly proposed legislation in Congress to reform habeas corpus by limiting the kinds of cases that gain review in federal courts. Although such efforts were supported by several presidential administrations, including Nixon's, Reagan's, and Bush's, until the mid-1990s Congress took few actions to block state prisoners from filing habeas petitions (Yackle 1993). Indeed, during congressional consideration of crime control legislation in 1994, with politicians from both political parties attempting to demonstrate to an aroused public their "toughness" on crime, neither house of Congress enacted habeas corpus reform in its version of the crime bill ("The Crime Bill" 1994). In 1996, Congress, for the first time, enacted legislation to place limits on habeas corpus. By that time, however, the Rehnquist Court had already moved ahead of Congress in initiating its own reforms of this statutorily defined area of law.

In the late 1980s, Chief Justice William Rehnquist made clear his desire to limit state prisoners' access to the federal courts and reduce the habeas corpus burden on the federal judiciary. Rehnquist appointed retired Justice Lewis Powell to head a committee to recommend reforms to streamline the processing of death penalty cases. Rehnquist submitted the Powell Committee's proposal to the Judicial Conference of the United States, the federal judges' policy-making body and the official body through which the judiciary communicates with Congress. Although a majority of judges on the Judicial Conference wanted to study the proposals and consider them at the Conference's next meeting a few months later, Rehnquist went ahead and submitted the proposals to Congress anyway. Rehnquist's action produced an unprecedented public rebuke when the *New York Times* reported that a majority of judges on the Judicial Conference sent a letter to Congress disassociating the Conference from Rehnquist's proposals for habeas corpus reform (Greenhouse 1989a).

Congress's unwillingness to enact reform legislation prior to 1996 did not leave Rehnquist and his like-minded colleagues helpless to pursue their stated goal of reducing the burden of habeas corpus petitions on the federal courts. In a series of decisions, the Supreme Court acted on its own to change habeas corpus procedures in ways that would limit state prisoners' access to review of their cases by federal judges (Alexander 1993). In 1989 in *Teague v. Lane,* for example, the Court announced that prisoners could not base habeas claims on new rules announced after their trials. Habeas petitions must be based on constitutional rights as defined by the Supreme Court at the time of the prisoner's conviction. They cannot be based on new Supreme Court decisions expanding the definitions of constitutional rights. According to Joseph Hoffmann (1989, 166), "*Teague* represents a watershed decision in the history of federal habeas...[because it] articulates a new vision of federal habeas that...will eventually reshape the entire area of the law." In effect, the federal courts can acknowledge that a prisoner's constitutional rights were violated. Despite such a finding, however, the courts will simultaneously decline to disturb that prisoner's conviction if the violated right was not fully recognized by a Supreme Court decision at the time the prisoner's case was adjudicated (*e.g., Butler v. McKellar* 1990). Moreover, the Rehnquist Court has defined the concept of "new rules" so broadly that "the Court's various descriptions of 'new rules' would seem to capture all claims raised in habeas corpus--claims seeking incremental developments in the content of legal standards and claims seeking the application of settled standards to different factual circumstances"

(Yackle 1993, 2391). The net result is a discernible movement toward federal court deference to state court decision making, even with regard to the protection of federal constitutional rights. Ironically, the Rehnquist Court is willing to apply new rules retroactively when they benefit the prosecution rather than the defendant as, for example, in cases concerning ineffective assistance of counsel (*Lockhart v. Fretwell* 1993).

Subsequent decisions produced additional limitations on prisoners' access to the federal courts. For example, in *McCleskey v. Zant* (1991) the Court limited the ability of prisoners to submit multiple habeas petitions. Thus Warren McCleskey was executed, despite his strong statistical evidence of systemic racial discrimination and despite the fact that prosecutors had sought to hide from his attorney evidence about a witness who was not identified to the jury as a police informer, evidence which two jurors declared would have led them to vote against imposition of the death penalty if they had known about it during the trial ("Warren McCleskey" 1991). The effort by McCleskey's lawyers to raise the latter claim was rejected by the Supreme Court and its decision served as a vehicle to create a new procedural rule demanding that all claims be asserted in a single petition.

The Court also mandated in *Coleman v. Thompson* (1991) that violations of state court procedures preclude review of petitioners' cases by the federal courts. In the latter case, an error by an attorney in filing an appeal even one day late can lead to complete forfeiture of all opportunities to have federal judges review the case for the existence of constitutional violations. Such rules emphasize efficient case processing over careful consideration of proper legal procedures. Moreover, such rules place into the hands of state judges, who are frequently elected officials closely tied to the local political environment, the final decision as to whether any *federal* constitutional rights violations existed. In other cases, the Court broadened the definition of harmless errors that need not be corrected and generally moved toward greater deference to "reasonable" judgments by state courts, even if those judgments were erroneous (Yackle 1993, 2408). As a result, the Supreme Court's decisions have raised concerns about the likelihood that defects in state court convictions will go undetected and, as a result, innocent people on death row may be unjustifiably executed (Smith and Jones 1993).

The judicial reform effort has also been advanced through use of other tools at the justices' disposal. For example, Chief Justice Rehnquist reassigned his colleagues to new jurisdictions as Circuit Justices. Prior to 1991, Justice Byron White had been the Circuit

Justice responsible for emergency petitions from the Fifth Circuit, which is comprised of Texas, Louisiana and Mississippi and is a source of a disproportionate number of death penalty cases. White routinely granted extensions for the filing deadlines facing prisoners who did not have the assistance of counsel in preparing their post-conviction claims. On Rehnquist's initiative, White was replaced by Justice Antonin Scalia who immediately announced that all prisoners must adhere to strict time limits for filing petitions, whether or not they have attorneys to assist them (Greenhouse 1991a). This policy increases the likelihood that some prisoners will forfeit their claims because they lack the knowledge, intellect, and literacy skills necessary to research, prepare, and present legal claims effectively (Smith 1987).

Judicial Workload as a Motivation for Reform

Advocates of habeas corpus reform, including Supreme Court justices, justify their objectives by citing the purportedly harmful impact of burdensome habeas corpus cases on the scarce time and resources of federal judicial officers. This is not the sole justification, because there are also federalism concerns about permitting state courts to handle and finalize their own cases (Greenhouse 1992). However, the impact of prisoners' petitions on the federal judicial workload has been portrayed by the justices as the primary justification.

The number of habeas cases rose dramatically between 1960 and the 1970s. According to Weisselberg (1990, 160), "New habeas corpus filings...increased sharply, beginning in the early 1960s....There was a steady rise in habeas corpus filings until fiscal year 1970, an overall decrease from fiscal year 1971 to fiscal year 1977, and then a steady increase to the most recent year." The number of filings rose from fewer than 1,000 petitions in 1960 to almost 9,000 petitions in the late 1970s to a steady caseload burden of nearly 13,000 cases each year in the early 1990s. Because habeas cases are seldom successful, they are often regarded as frivolous and duplicative ("Statistics Reflect" 1994). As a result, habeas cases, unlike some other categories of cases, are viewed as burdensome and expendable.

As Jim Thomas (1989) has demonstrated, however, denigrating characterizations of prisoners' petitions are frequently based on ideological perceptions and anecdotal evidence rather than on systematic analysis of the substance of prisoners' filings in the federal courts. Indeed, empirical studies of habeas corpus petitions conducted prior to the Supreme Court's recent reform initiatives raise questions about the accuracy of justices' perceptions about habeas cases. These studies indicated that many of the criticisms leveled at the purportedly abusive practices of habeas petitioners (i.e., failure to exhaust state remedies, not filing in a timely manner, and filing successive petitions) are readily explainable and less problematic than typically portrayed (Faust, Rubenstein, and Yackle 1991; Shapiro 1973).

Despite these questions about the nature of habeas cases and their actual impact on the workload of the federal courts, the perception that these cases are unnecessarily burdensome has surfaced in the comments of several of the justices whose decisions have created new procedural barriers to prisoners' petitions. For example, in his 1991 year-end report on the judicial branch, Chief Justice Rehnquist, who has openly advocated habeas reform, indicated his concerns about the burdens that these petitions place on the federal courts. According to Rehnquist (1992, 2), "Statutory habeas corpus procedures, particularly those dealing with capital cases, are also an area where careful reform can preserve the benefits of the Great Writ while rationalizing its application and eliminating the repetitive and time-intensive demands on the federal courts." Justice Sandra O'Connor (1981) also singled out habeas petitions for the burden of duplicative effort that they place on the federal courts by requiring review of cases already decided in state courts.

Justice Scalia has made a reduction in the caseload of the federal courts one of his primary crusades. In his first address to the American Bar Association, Scalia devoted his remarks to decrying the caseload burden experienced by the federal courts and recommending reforms that would remove from the courts what he characterized as "large categories of high volume, relatively routine cases" (Hengstler 1987). Because Scalia's caseload reduction efforts are not focused exclusively on prisoners' petitions, he uses the doctrine of standing and other means to block access to the federal courts for various kinds of cases (Brisbin 1990).

There is no question that the Supreme Court's efforts to reform habeas corpus procedures made it more difficult for prisoners to gain access to the federal courts and present petitions successfully. By creating new procedural rules through its judicial decisions, the Court has provided new grounds for decision makers in federal district courts to dismiss prisoners' petitions. As Sullivan (1993, 317) observed, "The trend in the Court's decisions is to elevate technical performance over substance in the evaluation of claims of federal rights violations."

Since the 1960s, critics of the Warren Court's decisions affecting criminal defendants' rights have sought to reduce the opportunities for state prisoners to bring their cases to federal court after failing to prevail in the state appellate courts. In the federal courts, typically fewer than one percent of habeas petitions are successful. A factor contributing to this lack of success is the fact that prisoners, who have no right to be represented by counsel, frequently violate procedural rules or fail to raise proper constitutional claims (Flango 1994). Because prisoners' habeas corpus petitions rarely survive dismissal in the federal courts, many critics believe that the federal courts' limited resources are wasted in reviewing the thousands of habeas petitions filed each year. These critics have included justices on the Rehnquist Court.

Although the Supreme Court possesses the motivation to reform habeas corpus procedures, and Congress possesses the clearest authority to effect significant reforms, there is strong reason to doubt that either policy-making institution is motivated solely by a desire to reduce the courts' workload. As Yackle (1993) has noted in reviewing the history of habeas reform initiatives, legislative and judicial advocates of reform frequently dress their twin desires to advance crime control and reduce the scope of criminal defendants' rights in the neutral clothing of court reform. The putative goal of preserving and protecting judicial institutions can obscure an underlying intention to limit opportunities for judicial review of convicted offenders' cases. In Yackle's (ibid., 2351) words, "the campaign to curtail habeas was not fueled primarily by an outcome-neutral concern that proper respect be shown to the state courts, nor by concerns about docket congestion."

The members of the Rehnquist Court who have initiated habeas corpus reform are the very same justices who have sought to reduce the scope of criminal defendants' rights established by Warren Court decisions. This observation is not meant to allege that a silent conspiracy exists. The justices are not necessarily seeking to reform habeas corpus in the name of protecting the federal judiciary when the actual purpose is to reduce the scope and availability of constitutional rights. In fact, some or all of these justices may genuinely believe that they have separated within their own minds their twin goals of reducing both judicial workloads and criminal defendants' rights. In practice, however, there is reason to doubt that judicial workload concerns alone provide a sufficient basis for habeas corpus reforms. A study of federal judicial officers found that the Rehnquist Court's reforms actually *increased* the workloads for U.S. Magistrate Judges who handle such cases in the district courts. Because of the Supreme Court's emphasis on creating procedural barriers to the filing of petitions, judicial officers spend more time reviewing procedural histories in cases than they would have spent deciding the claims on the merits (Smith 1995b). Thus the reforms limit the vindication of convicted offenders' constitutional rights but do not advance the putative goal of reducing judicial workloads.

If judicial workload were, indeed, the primary concern of the justices, then they should devote their attention and policy-making powers to other components of the federal caseload. Other categories of civil litigation and criminal cases obviously comprise much larger portions of the federal judicial caseload than do habeas corpus cases. In 1993, habeas petitions constituted only five percent of the 276,000 cases filed in federal district courts. Moreover, contrary to the impression that may be conveyed by the justices' statements and efforts concerning habeas corpus reform, seventy percent of all prisoners' cases in the federal courts are *not* habeas corpus petitions. Instead, these cases are civil rights lawsuits by prisoners. In 1995, there were 41,679 such prisoner lawsuits as compared to only 14,975 habeas corpus petitions (Maguire and Pastore 1996). Thus, the Court's reform efforts have been aimed at a relatively small class of cases.

Why would the Court target this category of cases that has a relatively small impact on the federal courts' caseload? After all, even the complete elimination of habeas corpus petitions would have a very modest impact on the federal courts' overall caseload and thousands of prisoners' civil rights lawsuits would remain on the docket. The Supreme Court's actions can be best understood in terms of dual motives rather than as the advancement of the single goal of reducing judicial workload.

If the justices are motivated by the dual policy objectives of both limiting the effectuation of criminal defendants' rights and reducing judicial workload, two factors make habeas corpus cases an attractive target for judicial reform initiatives. First, habeas corpus petitions typically affect a wider range of constitutional rights than do prisoners' civil rights lawsuits. In habeas corpus cases, convicted offenders are seeking their freedom by alleging violations of a variety of trial rights. By contrast, prisoners' civil rights lawsuits typically seek compensation for a violation of a narrower range of rights affecting the policies and practices of correctional institutions. The differences between these two kinds of legal actions filed by prisoners provide an incentive for justices to pursue dual purposes through habeas corpus reform.

Second, it is easier for the Court to initiate reforms of habeas corpus procedures than changes in civil rights laws. Both areas are governed by federal statutes, but judicial reinterpretation of civil rights laws affects a wider array of potential litigants, including many different categories of people throughout society (e.g., ethnic groups, gender groups, religious groups, etc). Congressional enactment of the Civil Rights Act of 1991, which responded to judicial decisions affecting employment discrimination law, provides strong evidence that Supreme Court decisions curtailing civil rights laws can generate effective opposition from other authoritative institutions. By contrast, habeas corpus laws are limited to people in government custody and therefore no powerful political constituency stands ready to combat judicial initiatives on habeas corpus. Thus, the Supreme Court has the opportunity to initiate habeas corpus reform with little risk that Congress will enact legislation to reverse the judicial action.

In the habeas corpus reform enacted by Congress, the Antiterrorism and Effective Death Penalty Act of 1996, new filing deadlines and limits on successive petitions were imposed. The statute also required greater deference by the federal courts to decisions made by state courts in criminal cases ("New Antiterrorism Law" 1996). The strict filing deadlines increase the likelihood that offenders will default their claims, especially because they often do not have lawyers who can help them prepare their petitions to make effective presentation of their constitutional claims. In addition, the mandated deference of federal to state courts will impose a difficult burden on prisoners seeking to gain federal court review (Reuben 1996). They must show by clear and convincing evidence that, except for a constitutional error at trial, they would not have been found guilty (Greenhouse 1996a). This is an extraordinarily difficult standard to meet and is, moreover, one that can sacrifice defendants' constitutional rights by failing to correct errors made in state courts.

President Clinton signed the bill into law on April 24, 1996, after the point at which the Supreme Court schedules arguments for their annual term. Observers presumed that the first opportunity to challenge the legality of the statute would be at the start of the next Supreme Court term in October. In a surprising move, however, on May 3rd the Rehnquist Court designated June 3rd as the date for scheduled oral arguments in a case challenging the statute. This short time frame deviated from the Court's usual scheduling processes, which normally involve finishing all oral arguments by April in order to complete all written opinions by the end of June. The surprise announcement also gave the parties in the case an unusually short time period in which to prepare arguments concerning an exceptionally important issue. The four most liberal justices, Stevens, Souter, Ginsburg, and Breyer, issued a dissenting opinion to accompany the order setting the date for oral arguments. These four dissenters objected to the haste with which the Court was approaching the case and they said it was "both unnecessary and profoundly unwise" for the Court to hear the case on an expedited basis (Greenhouse 1996b). The dissenters added, "Even if the majority were right that this petition squarely presents substantial constitutional questions about the power of Congress to limit this Court's jurisdiction, our consideration of them surely should be undertaken with utmost deliberation, rather than unseemly haste" (*Felker v. Turpin* I 1996). There had previously been rare occasions when the Supreme Court scheduled cases at the end of the term on an expedited basis, such as the Watergate tapes case in the 1970s that concerned the national constitutional crisis over President Richard Nixon's refusal to hand over evidence to the special prosecutor investigating the Nixon administration's misdeeds (*United States v. Nixon* 1974). However, habeas corpus reform would not appear to have the same significance as the looming impeachment and possible prosecution of a sitting president. Thus there was an appearance that the most conservative justices on the Rehnquist Court were so intent on limiting habeas corpus and accelerating the execution of death row inmates that they were hurrying to supply the quickest possible endorsement for the drastic legislative reforms.

Some observers speculated that even some conservative justices might actually oppose the new statute as a threat to the Supreme Court's jurisdiction, especially since an assistant attorney general for the State of Georgia argued that the legislation withdrew the high court's authority to free a convict or order a new trial after lower courts had already handled the matter (Labaton 1996). Ultimately the Rehnquist Court unanimously upheld the statute by interpreting it to preserve the high court's original jurisdiction to receive habeas petitions directly from prisoners who find themselves blocked by the statute from raising their claims in the lower federal courts (*Felker v. Turpin* II 1996). The more liberal justices, who had sometimes objected to their conservative colleagues' activism in reforming habeas corpus procedures by judicial decree, deferred to Congress as the appropriate authority to define habeas procedures. The conservative justices had an additional incentive to endorse the statute: it further advanced the goal of limiting habeas corpus petitions that they had sought in their judicial decisions for the preceding decade.

As a result, many habeas petitioners will find their hope for federal review resting on the slim prospect of the nation's highest court accepting their cases for decision. This is unlikely for two reasons. First, a majority of justices on the Rehnquist Court seem insensitive to violations of criminal defendants' constitutional rights. A primary objective pursued by several of these justices had been to eliminate opportunities for federal courts to review decisions by state courts in criminal cases. Second, the Rehnquist Court has made a concerted effort to hear fewer and fewer cases each year. The Court gave full hearings and decisions to only 75 cases in the 1995-96 term, less than half the number of cases decided by the Supreme Court only a decade earlier (Greenhouse 1996c). Such caseload control helps to advance the conservative justices' preference for reducing the federal judiciary's involvement in various policy issues. It seems unlikely that many habeas petitioners, a class of litigants whose interests have been under attack by many Rehnquist Court doctrines, will succeed in having their cases among the chosen few selected for decision by the high court.

SPEEDING THE PATH TO PUNISHMENT

The Rehnquist Court's eagerness to implement criminal punishments and the justices' diminished concern for careful legal proceedings was well illustrated in the case of Robert Alton Harris, the first person to be executed by California in more than two decades. Harris was executed in 1992 for the horrible murders of two youths (Kaplan and Wright 1990). Depending on one's view of the propriety of capital punishment, it can certainly be argued that Harris's ultimate fate achieved some measure of justice. Even in Harris's case, however, there were questions about the adequacy of his representation because of the omission of psychiatric evidence about the effects of child abuse and "fetal alcohol syndrome" which might have precluded imposition of capital punishment (Reinhardt 1992, 218). In any case, the final hours of Harris's path to execution reveal the extent to which the Rehnquist Court majority emphasizes efficiency and finality over careful consideration of legitimate legal issues.

As described by Judge Stephen Reinhardt (1992) of the U.S. Court of Appeals for the Ninth Circuit, the Governor of California rejected Harris's request for clemency. The next day a class action was filed alleging that the use of the gas chamber violated the constitutional prohibition against cruel and unusual punishments. This was a legitimate concern because California had not used the method in twenty-five years, so there was an issue about whether evolving Eighth Amendment standards, under the flexible approach applied by the Supreme Court since the *Trop* case in the 1950s, had now made this method of execution insufficiently humane for contemporary society. Moreover, the two other states that had used the gas chamber in recent decades, Mississippi and Arizona, had both reconsidered its use in reaction to actual gruesome applications. In the case of Arizona, the gas chamber was used only a week before Harris's scheduled execution and even the Attorney General of Arizona immediately recommended adoption of a different method after witnesses described the horrible scene (ibid., 218). In fact, the aftermath of Arizona's use of lethal gas provided a stronger, plausible basis for Harris's claim--a basis which would not have existed if he had raised the claim at an earlier point in his case.

The U.S. district judge issued a temporary restraining order to halt the scheduled execution until after she could review arguments and evidence regarding this claim. Although such orders are generally not appealable, the Ninth Circuit Court of Appeals three-judge panel that had previously considered other aspects of the Harris case agreed to consider California's request to overturn the district judge. The panel listened to a telephone conference call argument on the issues and subsequently gave Harris's attorneys 90 minutes to file a written brief before vacating the district judge's order. The appellate panel's two-to-one decision was based on the claim that the district judge's order was interfering with an ongoing state judicial proceeding, despite the fact that California proceedings in the case were over--except for carrying out the execution which was scheduled for later that same day.

Eleven other judges on the Ninth Circuit Court of Appeals found the panel's decision unacceptable and through electronic mail (e-mail) communications they called for an *en banc* reconsideration of the panel's action by a larger body of judges. Ten judges signed an order to stay the execution pending *en banc* consideration of the issue concerning Harris's class action cruel and unusual punishment claim (ibid., 210).

Meanwhile, in Washington, D.C., at six a.m. the following morning, the U.S. Supreme Court decided by a seven-to-two vote that lower federal courts could not consider the cruel and unusual punishment claim because it had not been raised by Harris in a previous habeas corpus petition (*Gomez v. United States District Court* 1992). Consistent with the judicial reform of habeas corpus described in the foregoing discussion, the Court emphasized the procedural details of when the issue was raised--too late, in the eyes of the majority, rather than the substance of the claim. However, the Court's habeas corpus reforms should not have applied to this case because the action concerned a civil rights lawsuit not governed by *McCleskey v. Zant* rather than a habeas corpus petition, which would be affected by the Court's reforms (Caminker and Chemerinsky 1992). Moreover, the Court's opinion emphasized that as a matter of equity, the legal concept roughly akin to "fairness" in the language of lay people, California would be inconvenienced by a requirement that they respond to such a claim raised so late in the legal process. There was, however, no discussion of the equity interest or fairness in executing Harris (and others) through the use of a method (i.e., the gas chamber) that judges in California and two justices on the Supreme Court (dissenters Stevens and Blackmun) believed deserved examination as a potentially inhumane and unconstitutional punishment (Reinhardt 1992, 212).

When the Supreme Court removed the stay of execution by the Ninth Circuit Court of Appeals, it was 3 a.m. in California. The federal appellate judges were asleep and had no access to the Supreme Court's opinion and reasoning. One of Harris' lawyers awoke one of the appellate judges with a telephone call. The lawyer informed the judge that the stay had been removed but noted that the original panel decision had declared that the *Harris* case should still be in state court beyond the reach of federal judicial intrusion. Thus the lawyer asked the federal judge to support the original panel order, which had effectively been restored by the Supreme Court's decision, by issuing a new stay of execution that would permit the attorneys to file an action in state court prior to imminent execution. The judge issued a twenty-four-hour stay in order to permit the lawyers to pursue their action in state instead of federal court in accordance with the now-restored decision by the panel that the case was still under state court control (ibid., 213).

The Rehnquist Court reacted swiftly. According to Judge Reinhardt (ibid.), the justices "immediately entered another order, one without precedent in our jurisprudence. The Supreme Court not only vacated [the judge's] order, but stripped all lower federal courts of their authority to act in the Harris case." Law professors Evan Caminker and Erwin Chemerinsky (1992, 246) labeled this aspect of the Supreme Court's order as "both extraordinary and unprecedented" because it "preclud[ed] lower [federal] courts from exercising powers expressly granted to them by congressional statutes." Although some commentators claimed that judges on the Ninth Circuit Court of Appeals were disobeying the Supreme Court because those judges oppose the death penalty, Reinhardt maintains that the judges were merely fulfilling their duties by delaying the execution until legitimate legal issues could be considered. Reinhardt concedes that Harris, or more accurately, Harris's lawyers could have raised the issue of cruel and unusual punishment earlier in the process (Reinhardt 1992, 219). However, the ultimate question is whether an execution should go forward, despite the existence of unresolved legal questions, merely to facilitate efficiency and finality in the legal process (ibid.):

The Supreme Court's moral values led it to conclude that delay by a lawyer outweighed any interest the defendant had in not being executed by cruel and unusual means. That is a moral value the Court is free to adopt. The question is, however, does that truly represent the moral values of this civilized nation?

In essence, it appears that the Rehnquist Court majority has grown impatient with delays affecting the implementation of capital punishment. As a result, according to Caminker and Chemerinsky, "this Court lately has become all too flippant with its unreflective accusations of litigant tardiness" (Caminker and Chemerinsky 1992, 240). In Harris's case, the last-minute nature of his cruel and unusual punishment claim received support from Arizona's experience and negative reaction to the reactivation of the gas chamber only one week earlier. All legal claims in the final hours are not necessarily frivolous. As Judge Reinhardt (1992, 220) notes,

> If there is no substance, no basis, to a defendant's last minute appeal, the federal courts are perfectly capable of dealing with the matter expeditiously. The district court can summarily reject a wholly meritless claim, and the circuit court can swiftly dispose of any frivolous appeal. There is no problem with any of that. However, no one contends that Harris' case was sham, that he didn't present a constitutional question of the first order.

The *Harris* case (*Harris v. Vazquez* 1992) shows the Rehnquist Court assuming a posture in which the justices "approached the final attempts to stay his execution with disdain and had no desire to consider (nor to let other courts consider) the merits of his claim. In their effort to ensure that death not be delayed, their legal opinions were quickly prepared and poorly reasoned" (Caminker and Chemerinsky 1992, 252). In their preoccupation with emphasizing the acceleration and finality of criminal punishments, the Rehnquist Court justices abdicated their responsibilities for ensuring that proper legal procedures are respected and that plausible constitutional claims receive appropriate scrutiny.

After Harris's execution, the federal district court had the opportunity to examine the Eighth Amendment claim originally raised by Harris. In the case, to which Harris's name was still attached, the district judge declared that California's use of execution by lethal gas violates the Eighth Amendment's prohibition on cruel and unusual punishments. The court's decision focused on the painful nature of execution in the gas chamber (*Fierro v. Gomez* 1994, 1404):

> [A]n inmate probably remains conscious anywhere from 15 seconds to one minute, and...there is a substantial likelihood that consciousness, or a waxing and waning of consciousness, persists for several additional minutes. During this time,...inmates suffer intense, visceral pain, primarily as a result of lack of oxygen to the cells. The experience of "air hunger" is akin to the experience of a major heart attack, or to being held under water. Other possible effects of the cyanide gas include tetany, an exquisitely painful contraction of the muscles, and painful build-up of lactic acid and adrenaline. Cyanide-induced cellular suffocation causes anxiety, panic, terror, and pain.

The U.S. Court of Appeals upheld the district court's decision (*Fierro v. Gomez* 1996) so it is possible the Rehnquist Court will have the opportunity to consider whether the gas chamber violates the Eighth Amendment.

THE CONSEQUENCES OF LIMITED ACCESS

The most jarring consequence of limited and inadequate access to judicial review of criminal cases is the risk that innocent people's convictions will never be reexamined and redressed. This risk has its most serious impact in capital cases. If a person in prison subsequently has his or her innocence established, the person can be released. Although a person cannot regain lost years of a life, life can be begun again. By contrast, in capital cases there can be no remedy for a life mistakenly extinguished. Between 1980 and 1993, there were reportedly twenty-one death-row inmates who gained release because of evidence that proved their innocence ("Tests Clear Man" 1993). Many of these innocent people would have been executed if the Rehnquist Court's legal procedure decisions had been fully developed and implemented in the years immediately following their erroneous convictions.

James Richardson was sentenced to death in Florida for poisoning his seven children in 1967. The prosecution claimed that the illiterate farm worker killed his own children to collect the insurance money, even though the prosecutors knew that there was no insurance policy on the children. After twenty-one years in prison, Richardson was released when supporters discovered evidence of prosecutorial misconduct and evidence emerged that pointed to the children's babysitter as the culprit (Baker 1989).

Randall Adams was sentenced to death in Texas for shooting a police officer during a traffic stop in 1976. Adams was an unemployed man who moved to Texas in search of work. The prime witness against him was a teenager with a serious criminal record whom Adams had befriended. When a documentary filmmaker investigated Adams' case in the late 1980s and made it the focus of his award-winning film, *The Thin Blue Line*, inconsistencies in witnesses' testimony emerged and the teenage star witness, now an adult on death row after conviction for a subsequent 1985 murder, admitted that he killed the officer when Adams was not even present (Gallagher 1989). Eventually Adams was released after serving twelve years on death row.

In other examples, Walter McMillian spent nearly five years on death row in Alabama for murdering a teenage dry cleaning clerk during a robbery. He was released in 1993 when even the prosecutors conceded that the three witnesses who placed him at the scene had done so either to collect reward money or to deflect attention from their own guilt (Mitchell 1993). Kirk Bloodworth spent nine years in prison, including several on death row, in Maryland for a rape-murder before a reexamination of physical evidence and newly developed DNA testing demonstrated that he was not guilty ("Tests Clear Man" 1993). He gained his release in 1993. In 1996, three Illinois men were released from prison, including two who had been waiting for execution on death row, after being incarcerated for eighteen years for a murder that they did not commit. New DNA evidence and a confession by another man provided the basis for discovering the errors that had led to their convictions (Terry 1996). If accelerated appeal and habeas corpus processes had been in place, these innocent men could very well have been executed for crimes that they did not commit.

There is nothing novel in the recognition that the American justice system is fallible and that mistakes will inevitably occur. Indeed, some might point to these cases as examples of the system's success and strength because errors were corrected through the release of wrongly convicted, innocent people. The more important point, however, is the necessity of having review processes available to correct the system's errors. As the *New York Times* noted about McMillian's case (Applebome 1993, A1),

> If the jury's sentence of life in prison without parole had been left in place, Mr. McMillian might have been another forgotten black inmate in an Alabama

prison. But Judge Key overruled the jury and condemned Mr. McMillian to die in the electric chair. Because of the death sentence, Mr. McMillian's case was vigorously appealed, and the truth came out.

Because of the Rehnquist Court's efforts to accelerate reviews of capital cases and block access to the federal judiciary when lawyers make procedural errors, other wrongly convicted inmates might not have the opportunity to have their cases reexamined. Such cases may already have arisen.

In *Butler v. McKellar* (1990), the Supreme Court refused to give retroactive application to a decision concerning a defendant's rights during police interrogation. In effect, the justices conceded that Butler's rights were violated when the police initiated interrogation sessions with him outside of the presence of his attorney, but under their broad definition of "new rules" in the habeas corpus process, they refused to grant Butler a new trial despite the acknowledgement of the improper actions by the police. A *Washington Post* investigation raised serious questions about Horace Butler's guilt in the rape-murder case. Butler's inexperienced attorney never had his client's mental capacity tested. Thus the jury never learned that Butler had the mental functioning of a nine-year-old with an IQ of 61 and had never even completed the third grade. Indeed, the prosecutor later stated that he never would have sought the death penalty if he had known that Butler was mentally retarded (Marcus 1990, 12). This fact alone should call into question Butler's capacity to waive his right to counsel during police-initiated questioning at the jail. Moreover, an FBI agent determined that pubic hairs found on the victim's clothing were definitely not from Butler (ibid.). Because the Supreme Court blocked further federal judicial review of Butler's case, he stayed on death row with no comprehension of what had happened to him (ibid). Despite the acknowledged violation of his constitutional rights that contributed to his conviction, the Supreme Court's emphasis on efficiency and finality in implementing criminal punishments prevented any federal court from vindicating Butler's rights.

In another case (*O'Dell v. Thompson* 1991), a man was convicted of murder based on circumstantial evidence and blood typing tests indicating that blood on his clothes matched the victim's blood type. When new kinds of blood testing techniques based on DNA analysis were later developed, it was shown that the victim's blood did not match the genetic composition of the blood on his clothing. However, he had no opportunity to seek federal judicial review of his conviction.

He was barred by the Rehnquist Court's *Coleman* rule because his attorney made a procedural error by filing the wrong document (Greenhouse 1991b).

The problem of erroneous decisions is potentially exacerbated by the viewpoint expressed by several Rehnquist Court justices that the post-trial presentation of evidence showing actual innocence does not justify the intervention of a federal court to order a new trial. When Chief Justice Rehnquist writes that "Claims of actual innocence based on newly discovered evidence have never been held to state a ground for federal habeas relief absent an independent constitutional violation occurring in the underlying state criminal proceeding" (*Herrera v. Collins* 1993, 400), it implies that the execution of an innocent person would not violate any constitutional rights. Justice Scalia echoed this message by declaring that "there is no basis in text, tradition, or even in contemporary practice (if that were enough), for finding in the Constitution a right to demand judicial consideration of newly discovered evidence of innocence brought forward after conviction" (ibid., 427). These justices justify the abdication of judicial involvement in such circumstances by trusting that elected officials, especially governors, will intervene to insure that injustices do not occur. According to Rehnquist (ibid., 411), "History shows that the traditional remedy for claims of innocence based on new evidence, discovered too late in the day to file a new trial motion, has been executive clemency." The tradition of judicial protection of individual rights as well as the life tenure granted to federal judges seem well suited to empower the judicial branch to protect the rights of individuals against abuses undertaken by officials in law enforcement and prosecution, two functions controlled by the executive branch. Thus, it seems odd to trust elected executive branch officials, who must cater to the public's whims in order to gain reelection, to identify and correct errors for which their subordinates are responsible.

The foregoing examples of errors and possible errors by the justice system are not unique. Michael Radelet, Hugo Bedeau, and Constance Putnam (1992) have documented troubling errors in more than 400 murder and rape cases during the twentieth century in which the convictions of apparently innocent people raised the spectre of the most severe criminal punishments being erroneously applied. Because the human decision making that underlies the criminal justice process makes the process inherently fallible, it is troubling that the mechanisms for correcting errors are eroding and disappearing in the hands of the Rehnquist Court. Moreover, Chief Justice Rehnquist (1989) has said that "The Supreme Court of the United States should be reserved...for important and disputed questions of law, not for individual injustices that might be corrected and should be corrected in other courts." Even if one agrees with Rehnquist's view that the Supreme Court should not be responsible for correcting individual injustices, how can the other courts, which in Rehnquist's view bear that responsibility, carry out this task if the nation's highest court persists in creating new procedural barriers to the presentation of claims for judicial examination?

CONCLUSION

The imposition of criminal punishment is determined, in part, by the availability and implementation of rights and procedures which ensure that defendants receive the benefits of the fair processes due them under the American constitutional system. The decisions of the Rehnquist Court indicate that the protection of due process and constitutional rights is being eclipsed by values and policy preferences favoring swift and efficient implementation of punishment. The adversarial process is more slogan than reality in many criminal proceedings, yet the Supreme Court's decisions have weakened rather than strengthened the substantive meaning of the right to counsel. Moreover, the statutory mechanisms for gaining post-conviction reviews of alleged constitutional violations have been significantly restricted by decisions imposing judicial reforms upon the habeas corpus process. Although the justices have protected access to habeas corpus in some contexts (*O'Neal v. McAninch* 1995; *Schlup v. Delo* 1995), many decisions have significantly narrowed opportunities to gain federal judicial review of criminal convictions because of the creation and imposition of strict procedural rules. As a result of the justices' apparent eagerness to see criminal punishment imposed with little interference by post-trial federal judicial proceedings, there are risks that constitutional rights and due process are being inadequately protected. In the worst case situations, an emphasis on efficiency and finality will inevitably place certain unlucky--and innocent--individuals needlessly at risk for their lives in accelerated capital punishment proceedings.

CHAPTER 5

Conclusion

The protection of individual rights is an important responsibility of the judicial branch of government. The rights enjoyed by Americans have been defined, communicated to the public, and interposed as limitations upon government largely through judicial decisions. The judiciary is not solely responsible for the protection of rights because Americans expect officials in the legislative and executive branches to give due consideration to the Constitution in formulating and implementing public policies. Moreover, the actualization of individuals' rights rests largely in the hands of government officials, such as police officers, prosecutors, and judges, who must obey constitutional doctrines in making decisions about and interacting with citizens in order to make rights a reality. Although the judicial branch does not have exclusive control over the existence and implementation of rights, it provides the symbolic and substantive impetus for maintaining constitutional rights as treasured and protected entitlements.

Within the realm of constitutional rights, those that affect the criminal justice process are especially important. Because the control of crime is a governmental responsibility that is the focus of political controversy and public pressure, it is difficult for the officials empowered to investigate and prosecute crimes to single-handedly and self-consciously strike appropriate balances between fighting crime and protecting the rights of individual suspects. The U.S. Supreme Court has played an important role in defining the rights possessed by the most despised of political minorities, namely criminal offenders, while periodically reminding the public and justice officials that those same rights are needed to protect the average innocent citizen against the risk of abusive actions by government. The government possesses the awesome power to deprive individual citizens of their liberty and even their lives as punishment for criminal offenses. Such powers are often misused in other countries as a means to protect and perpetuate the power of political elites against threats by public opposition and rival oligarchic factions (Mandela 1994). Indeed, the tendency of those in power to use the criminal process for political preservation is amply demonstrated in American history, too, by the attempted suppression and harassment of civil rights advocates and by other examples of political minorities who endured prosecution and punishment as the price for asserting their viewpoints (Williams 1987).

Consistent with the conservative philosophical orientations of the justices who numerically dominate the Rehnquist Court, the nation's highest court has limited the scope of individuals' constitutional protections relevant to criminal punishment. In addressing prison conditions, the justices have imposed a relaxed standard of judicial scrutiny that focuses on corrections officials' intentions rather than simply on the actual habitability of prisons. With respect to capital punishment, the Rehnquist Court has clarified the scope of the death penalty by permitting executions for crimes committed by teenagers and mentally retarded people and by barring systemic equal protection challenges that rely on statistical evidence. The effect of such decisions is to provide significant flexibility for states and their criminal justice officials to pursue with few judicial impediments their own policy preferences in the design and implementation of punishment. At the same time, the Court has turned a blind eye toward the documented risk of discriminatory outcomes that are the inevitable products of cumulative discretionary decisions in prosecution and sentencing processes.

The Rehnquist Court's decisions affecting criminal punishment do not support simplistic characterizations of the high court's conservatism as inevitably producing support for the government when claims are asserted by individuals. In prison conditions cases, the Court surprised some observers by recognizing as colorable claims inmates' assertions about beatings that did not produce significant injuries (*Hudson v. McMillian* 1992), confinement of non-smoking inmates in cells with smokers (*Helling v. McKinney* 1993), and other forms of harm which are allegedly the products of either intention or deliberate indifference (*Farmer v. Brennan* 1994). The Court has also sided with defendants in noting improper weighing of factors in capital cases (*Sochor v. Florida* 1992). These examples demonstrate that the Rehnquist Court clearly acknowledged the continuing existence of constitutional rights, albeit less expansive ones than before, to protect individuals facing criminal punishment.

The Court's periodic expressions of support for the continuing existence of rights may conflict with critical characterizations of the Rehnquist Court as unrelentingly conservative. In light of the Rehnquist-era justices' overall record of decision making on punishment issues, however, the Court's declarations are akin to symbolic acknowledgements of rights' importance rather than the actual enforcement of substantive protections for defendants and convicted offenders. To borrow a phrase from Larry Yackle (1993, 2397), "What the Court hesitates to do wholesale, it may be perfectly willing to do retail." As the Court periodically endorses the existence of rights affecting criminal punishment and other aspects of criminal justice, it simultaneously constricts the opportunities for those rights to be recognized and vindicated by the federal courts. The entire thrust of the Court's habeas corpus reform is to block convicted offenders from seeking federal judicial review of alleged violations of their constitutional rights. The prohibition on raising issues under broadly defined "new rules" when linked with the Court's trend toward deference to "reasonable" yet potentially erroneous state court judgments creates a powerful barrier to federal judicial vindication of rights in criminal cases. According to Yackle (ibid.),

> The Justices who now seem ready to adopt a general
> deference rule clearly think that the "new rule"
> cases mean, at least in effect, that the federal
> courts must accept "reasonable" state judgments
> across the board. And even the Justices who refuse
> to shape the "new rule" cases into a general rule
> of deference [to state court judgments] may reach
> the same result on a case-by-case basis.

Capital punishment cases are affected by these barriers to habeas corpus petitions as well as by the Court's lack of attention to insuring a meaningful right to counsel under the Sixth Amendment. As a result, the states' increasing freedom to impose the death penalty produces greater risks of unremedied discrimination and errors.

Although the Court declined to accept Justice Scalia's argument that the Eighth Amendment contains no proportionality requirement, the justices' acceptance of a mandatory life sentence without parole for the drug offense in *Harmelin v. Michigan* (1991) leaves open the question of the extent to which non-capital punishments would actually be declared unconstitutionally disproportionate. The increasing political popularity of "three-strikes-and-you're-out" repeat offender sentencing laws makes future proportionality claims inevitable. Under these laws, offenders receive life sentences upon conviction for a third felony, whether or not it involved a violent offense. Thus people have received life sentences for theft offenses that would otherwise draw short sentences or probation. However, there is no indication that the Supreme Court would limit the application of such laws, especially since the Court's Rehnquist-era composition was more conservative than when the high court narrowly rejected a mandatory life sentence law in 1983 (*Solem v. Helm* 1983).

In prison conditions cases, notwithstanding the Court's recognition of colorable claims, the subjective standard adopted in *Wilson v. Seiter* (1991) may undercut judicial intervention into all but the most egregious examples of clearly recognizable Eighth Amendment violations. The real impact of *Wilson* will depend on how the lower federal courts interpret and apply the precedent. As Michael Mushlin (1993) has documented in analyzing relevant cases, it is quite clear throughout the Rehnquist Court's decisions concerning prisoners' rights that the high court expects significant judicial deference to the discretionary decisions of professional correctional administrators (*e.g., O'Lone v. Estate of Shabazz* 1987).

Contemporary conceptions of the U.S. Supreme Court's role in the American governing system were, in many ways, shaped by the actions of the Warren Court era. The public envisions the Warren-style Court as the institutional guardian of the Constitution. Meanwhile the justices appointed since the Warren era have continuously reacted against their predecessors' opinions in making decisions about constitutional issues. With respect to criminal punishment and other criminal justice issues, these reactions have generally limited the scope of individuals' rights and provided greater judicial deference to the policies and practices of government officials.

In the eyes of many Americans, there is a retrospective public image of the Warren Court justices admirably weathering adverse political reactions in standing firm behind *popular* pronouncements that condemned and delegitimized government-sponsored racial segregation (*Brown v. Board of Education* 1954) and provided attorneys for poor defendants who would have otherwise been helpless in the judicial process (*Gideon v. Wainwright* 1963). This image of the Court reinforces the popular notion that it is the job of the Supreme Court to protect and defend constitutional rights. Simultaneously, however, the Warren Court was also unpopular when it issued decisions with which many people disagreed. As David O'Brien (1990, 370) observes, "the Court sometimes invites controversy by challenging majoritarian sentiments to respect the rights of minorities and the principles of representative democracy." The Court's decisions supporting rights for criminal defendants were, with the probable exception of the popular *Gideon* case, a primary source of negative views about the high court in public opinion polls (Wasby 1988, 346).

When the Court's decisions comport with citizens' viewpoints, then the high court is appreciated and revered. When the Court is out of step with public opinion, however, there is likely to be continuing criticism of the Court's actions unless, as in the case of racial segregation, the public's views change and become more like those of the Court. Because the nation's "crime problem" became an entrenched preoccupation of the news media, politicians, and the public in the second half of the twentieth century, it is unlikely that the high court will receive public gratitude for any decisions favoring broad constitutional rights that benefit suspects, defendants, and convicted offenders as well as the general public. Thus the Rehnquist Court's decisional trends favoring finality, efficiency, and deference to criminal justice officials at the expense of constitutional protections are not out of step with the mood of the American public.

This is not to say, however, that the details of the Rehnquist Court's decisions affecting criminal punishment would necessarily receive broad public support. It is unlikely that the public would endorse practices that lead innocent people to be convicted of murder and sentenced to death. News media attention to the discovery of such erroneous convictions (*e.g.,* Willwerth 1993; "Tests Clear Man" 1993; Colford 1993; Baker 1989; Gallagher 1989) and to the unequal resources available to poor defendants (*e.g.,* Kaplan 1994; Smolowe 1993; Lacayo 1992) are regular features of investigative journalism designed to shock the public's conscience (and sell newspapers and news magazines). While these stories may enhance public disappointment in the justice system, there are two reasons that they are unlikely to generate opposition to the Supreme Court's decisions. First, the public receives relatively little information about Supreme Court decisions and much of that information consists of inaccurate characterizations contained in "snippets" about high court decisions on television news programs (Slotnick and Segal 1994). Second, most of the Rehnquist Court's actions that have contributed to or failed to remedy these problems are obscured in relatively arcane decisions about habeas corpus procedures. The public is not unhappy to hear that the Supreme Court is streamlining procedures for implementing punishment because they have little opportunity to see how those new procedures limit the protection of constitutional rights and contribute to errors and unequal justice. Perhaps public opinion supports the general notion that "criminals have too many rights," and therefore the Rehnquist Court's decisions are consistent with predominant contemporary beliefs and values. Even so, the specific impacts of the Court's decisions are obscured from view and therefore public recognition, scrutiny, and debate of such issues are impeded by the path that the justices have chosen to advance their preference for narrower constitutional rights.

Whether or not the Rehnquist Court's decisions would, if fully understood, enjoy broad public support, the high court's decisions affecting criminal punishment raise questions about the judicial branch's role and responsibilities in the constitutional governing system. For most of American history, the Supreme Court provided relatively little support for individuals who brought forward allegations of constitutional violations by government. During the mid-twentieth century, the Court redefined its focus and role by emphasizing the interpretation and protection of individuals' constitutional rights (Baum 1992). The Rehnquist Court still faces many questions about civil rights and liberties. While the Rehnquist Court has not abandoned all responsibilities for protecting rights, its narrow conception of rights and disinclination to permit federal judicial intrusion into state courts and governing institutions has effectively altered the high court's assertions of authority and its role in protecting individuals' rights.

This diminution of constitutional protection for individuals is especially evident in criminal justice cases, just as it has been since the Burger Court years of the 1970s. In a Burger Court decision rejecting First Amendment and equal protection claims by prisoners, Justices Thurgood Marshall and William Brennan warned that the Court's approach to analyzing prisoners' claims would soon result in the elimination of most constitutional rights for convicted offenders. In Marshall's words (*Jones v. North Carolina Prisoners' Labor Union* 1977, 147),

> If the mode of analysis adopted in today's decision were to be generally followed, prisoners eventually would be stripped of all constitutional rights, and would retain only those privileges that prison officials, in their informed discretion, deigned to recognize. The sole constitutional constraint on prison officials would be a requirement that they act rationally. Ironically, prisoners would be left with a right of access to the courts,...but no substantive rights to assert once they get there.

Marshall's worst-case scenario was not fulfilled because the Supreme Court has continued to acknowledge various rights for defendants and convicted offenders. However, his words had a prophetic quality as the Rehnquist Court emphasized deference to correctional officials even more strongly than the Burger Court majority. Moreover, the judicially initiated reform of habeas corpus and the limitation on systemic remedies for deficient prison law libraries made the effective right of access to the federal courts a distant memory for many habeas corpus petitioners. In light of the astounding growth in American prison populations, from less than 330,000 in 1980 to nearly 1.1 million in 1994, and the attendant consequences of overcrowded conditions and other problems, the lasting legacy of Rehnquist Court jurisprudence remains to be evaluated. Because Congress took aggressive actions in 1996 to limit opportunities for prison reform litigation and to erect barriers to federal judicial review of habeas corpus petitions, there are strong reasons for the Supreme Court to be especially vigilant in safeguarding constitutional rights. There is no indication, however, that the Rehnquist Court is inclined to assume this responsibility. Perhaps the Warren and Burger Court era decisions that pushed police officers, prosecutors, judges, and corrections officials to professionalize their operations will provide a continuing level of practical protection for citizens drawn into the criminal justice system. Alternatively, however, the Rehnquist Court's efforts to reduce federal judicial supervision of the criminal justice system may eventually turn back the clock to a time when criminal justice officials determined people's fates through discretionary decisions that were beyond the interest and reach of the branch of government empowered to interpret and defend constitutional rights.

References

Abraham, Henry J. 1985. *Justices and Presidents: A Political History of Appointments to the Supreme Court*, 2nd ed. New York: Oxford University Press.

———. 1988. *Freedom and the Court*, 5th ed. New York: Oxford University Press.

Acker, James R. 1993. "A Different Agenda: The Supreme Court, Empirical Research, Evidence, and Capital Punishment Decisions, 1986-1989." *Law and Society Review* 27: 65-88.

Alderman, Ellen and Caroline Kennedy. 1991. *In Our Defense: The Bill of Rights in Action*. New York: William Morrow.

Alexander, Rudolph, Jr. "The Demise of State Prisoners' Access to Federal Habeas Corpus." *Criminal Justice Policy Review* 6: 55-70.

Applebome, Peter. 1992. "Indigent Defendants, Overworked Lawyers." *New York Times*, 17 May, E18.

———. 1993. "Black Man Freed After Years on Death Row in Alabama." *New York Times*, 3 March, A1.

Baker, James N. 1989. "From Tragedy to Travesty." *Newsweek*, 24 April, 68.

Barrett, Paul M. 1994. "Lawyer's Fast Work on Death Cases Raises Doubts About System." *Wall Street Journal*, 7 September.

Baugh, Joyce A., Christopher E. Smith, Thomas R. Hensley, and Scott Patrick Johnson. 1994. "Justice Ruth Bader Ginsburg: A Preliminary Assessment." *University of Toledo Law Review* 26: 1-34.

Baum, Lawrence. 1992. *The Supreme Court*, 4th ed. Washington, DC: Congressional Quarterly Press.

Beck, Allen J. and Darrell K. Gilliard. 1995. "Prisoners in 1994." *Bureau of Justice Statistics Bulletin* (August).

Berkson, Larry Charles. 1975. *The Concept of Cruel and Unusual Punishment*. Lexington, MA: Lexington Books.

Blasecki, Janet L. 1990. "Justice Lewis Powell: Swing Voter or Staunch Conservative?" *Journal of Politics* 52: 530-547.

Bodenhamer, David J. 1992. *Fair Trial: Rights of the Accused in American History*. New York: Oxford University Press.

Bork, Robert H. 1990. *The Tempting of America: The Political Seduction of Law*. New York: Basic Books.

Bowers, William J. 1983. "The Pervasiveness of Arbitrariness and Discrimination Under Post-*Furman* Statutes." *Journal of Criminal Law and Criminology* 74: 1067-1100.

Brennan, William J. 1987. "The Constitution of the United States: Contemporary Ratification." In *American Constitutional Law*, 8th ed., eds. A. Mason and D. Stephenson. Englewood Cliffs, NJ: Prentice-Hall.

Brigham, John. 1987. *The Cult of the Court*. Philadelphia: Temple University Press.

Bright, Stephen B. 1994. "Counsel for the Poor: The Sentence Not for the Worst Crime but for the Worst Lawyer." *Yale Law Journal* 103: 1835-1883.

Bright, Stephen B., Stephen O. Kinnard, and David A. Webster. 1990. "Keeping *Gideon* from Being Blown Away." *Criminal Justice* (Winter): 11-13, 46-48.

Brisbin, Richard A., Jr. 1990. "The Conservatism of Antonin Scalia." *Political Science Quarterly* 105: 1-29.

Call, Jack E. 1995. "The Supreme Court and Prisoners' Rights." *Federal Probation* 59 (March): 36-46.

Caminker, Evan and Erwin Chemerinsky. 1992. "The Lawless Execution of Robert Alton Harris." *Yale Law Journal* 102: 225-253.

"Canada Court: Michigan's Prison Sentences Shocking." 1994. *The State News* (Michigan State University), 14 September, 2.

Canon, Bradley. 1983. "Defining the Dimensions of Judicial Activism." *Judicature* 66: 236-247.

Case Comment. 1983. "Eighth Amendment Prohibits Imposition of Death Penalty on Accomplice to a Felony Murder." *Washington University Law Quarterly* 61: 253-259.

"Casenote, *Tison v. Arizona*: Justice O'Connor Creates a New Standard for Capital Crimes." 1987. *Creighton Law Review* 21: 359-379.

Cohen, Adam. 1995. "The Difference a Million Makes." *Time*, 29 March, 43.

Cole, George F. 1995. *The American System of Criminal Justice*, 7th ed. Belmont, CA: Wadsworth Publishing.

Colford, Christopher. 1993. "Cruel, But Not Unusual, Mistakes." *Cleveland Plain Dealer*, 7 March, 3-C.

Cook, Julian A., Jr. and Mark S. Kende. 1996. "Colorblindness in the Rehnquist Court: Comparing the Court's Treatment of Discrimination Claims by a Black Death Row Inmate and White Voting Rights Plaintiffs." *Cooley Law Review* 13: 815-852.

Cox, Archibald. 1968. *The Warren Court: Constitutional Decision as an Instrument of Reform*. Cambridge, MA: Harvard University Press.

Coyle, Marcia. 1990a. "Counsel's Guiding Hand Is Often Handicapped by the System It Serves." *National Law Journal*, 11 June, 36.

_____. 1990b. "A Triple Whammy Here (in Louisiana) Foils Real Justice." *National Law Journal*, 11 June, 36.

"The Crime Bill Moves Through House." *The Third Branch* 26 (May): 1-3.

Danelski, David J. 1989. "The Influence of the Chief Justice in the Decisional Process of the Supreme Court." In *American Court Systems*, 2nd ed., eds. S. Goldman and A. Sarat. New York: Longman.

Davis, Sue. 1989. *Justice Rehnquist and the Constitution*. Princeton, NJ: Princeton University Press.

Decker, John F. 1992. *Revolution to the Right: Criminal Procedure Jurisprudence during the Burger-Rehnquist Court Era*. New York: Garland Publishing.

Dorin, Dennis D. 1994. "Far Right of the Mainstream: Racism, Rights, and Remedies From the Perspective of Justice Antonin Scalia's *McCleskey* Memorandum." *Mercer Law Review* 45: 1035-1088.

Douglas, William O. 1974. *Go East, Young Man*. New York: Random House.

Eisler, Kim Isaac. 1993. *A Justice For All: William J. Brennan and the Decisions That Transformed America*. New York: Simon & Schuster.

Epstein, Lee and Joseph F. Kobylka. 1992. *The Supreme Court and Legal Change: Abortion and the Death Penalty*. Chapel Hill, NC: University of North Carolina Press.

Epstein, Lee and Thomas G. Walker. 1992. *Constitutional Law for a Changing America: Rights, Liberties, and Justice*. Washington, DC: Congressional Quarterly Press.

Faust, Richard, Tina J. Rubenstein, and Larry W. Yackle. 1991. "The Great Writ in Action: Empirical Light on the Federal Habeas Corpus Debate." *New York University Review of Law and Social Change* 18: 637-710.

Fedarko, Kevin. 1995. "A Gun Ban Is Shot Down." *Time*, 8 May, 85.

Feeley, Malcolm. 1989. "The Significance of Prison Conditions Cases: Budgets and Regions." *Law and Society Review* 23: 273-282.

Flango, Victor E. 1994. *Habeas Corpus in State and Federal Courts*. Williamsburg, VA: National Center for State Courts.

Friedelbaum, Stanley H. 1994. *The Rehnquist Court: In Pursuit of Judicial Conservatism*. Westport, CT: Praeger Publishers.

Friedman, Lawrence M. 1993. *Crime and Punishment in American History*. New York: Basic Books.

Gallagher, John E. 1989. "No Happy Ending." *Time*, 6 March, 56.

Garcia, Alfredo. 1992. *The Sixth Amendment in Modern American Jurisprudence*. Westport, CT: Greenwood.

Gershman, Bennett L. 1993. "Themes of Injustice: Wrongful Conviction, Racial Prejudice, and Lawyer Incompetence." *Criminal Law Bulletin* 29: 502-515.

Gey, Steven G. 1992. "Justice Scalia's Death Penalty." *Florida State University Law Review* 20: 67-132.

Gibson, James L. 1983. "From Simplicity to Complexity: The Development of Theory in the Study of Judicial Behavior." *Political Behavior* 5: 7-49.

Gleick, Elizabeth. 1995. "Rich Justice, Poor Justice." *Time*, 19 June, 38.

Greenhouse, Linda. 1989a. "Judges Challenge Rehnquist's Role on Death Penalty: An Extraordinary Move." *New York Times*, 6 October, A1.

_____. 1989b. "Rights of Death Row Inmates to Legal Assistance Are Limited." *New York Times*, 24 June, 8.

_____. 1990. "An Activist's Legacy." *New York Times*, 22 July, 1, 22.

_____. 1991a. "Scalia Tightens Policy on Death Penalty Appeals." *New York Times*, 22 February, B16.

_____. 1991b. "In Shift, O'Connor Urges Appeal in Murder Case." *New York Times*, 3 December, B10.

_____. 1992. "A Window on the Court: Justices Take an Assertive Role to Reduce Habeas Corpus Petitions by State Inmates." *New York Times*, 6 May, A1, A20.

_____. 1996a. "Justices to Consider Inmates' Access to Courts." *New York Times*, 3 June (from New York Times World Wide Web site: www.nytimes.com).

_____. 1996b. "Justices, With Unusual Speed, Agree to Review New U.S. Law." *New York Times*, 4 May (from New York Times World Wide Web site: www.nytimes.com).

_____. 1996c. "In Supreme Court's Decisions, a Clear Voice, and a Murmur." *New York Times*, 3 July, A12.

Gross, Samuel R. 1996. "The Risks of Death: Sources of Error in Capital Prosecutions." *Buffalo Law Review* 44: 469-500.

Gross, Samuel R. and Robert Mauro. 1984. "Patterns of Death: An Analysis of Racial Disparities in Capital Sentencing and Homicide Victimization." *Stanford Law Review* 37: 27-153.

Hengstler, Gary A. 1987. "Scalia Seeks Court Change." *ABA Journal* 73 (April): 20.

Hirsch, H.N. 1981. *The Enigma of Felix Frankfurter*. New York: Basic Books.

Hoffmann, Joseph L. 1989. "The Supreme Court's New Vision of Federal Habeas Corpus for State Prisoners." *Supreme Court Review* (1989): 165-194.

_____. 1993. "The 'Cruel and Unusual Punishment Clause': A Limit on the Power to Punish or Constitutional Rhetoric?" In *The Bill of Rights in Modern America: After 200 Years*, eds. D. Bodenhamer and J. Ely. Bloomington, IN: Indiana University Press.

Johnson, Charles A. and Bradley C. Canon. 1984. *Judicial Politics: Implementation and Impact*. Washington, DC: Congressional Quarterly Press.

Johnson, Scott P. and Christopher E. Smith. 1992. "David Souter's First Term on the Supreme Court: The Impact of a New Justice." *Judicature* 75: 238-242.

Kairys, David J. 1993. *With Liberty and Justice for Some*. New York: New Press.

Kamisar, Yale. 1983. "The Warren Court (Was It Really So Defense-Minded?), The Burger Court (Is It Really so Prosecution-Oriented?), and Policy Investigatory Practices." In *The Burger Court: The Counter-Revolution That Wasn't*, ed. V. Blasi. New Haven, CT: Yale University Press.

_____. 1987. "The 'Police Practice' Phases of the Criminal Process and the Three Phases of the Burger Court." In *The Burger Years: Rights and Wrongs in the Supreme Court, 1969-1986*, ed. H. Schwartz. New York: Penguin.

Kannar, George. 1990. "The Constitutional Catechism of Antonin Scalia." *Yale Law Journal* 99: 1297-1357.

Kaplan, David A. 1994. "Catch-22 at the High Court." *Newsweek*, 11 April, 68.

Kaplan, David A. and Bob Cohn. 1991. "These Clients Aren't Fools." *Newsweek*, 22 April, 66.

Kaplan, David A. and Lynda Wright. 1990. "Breaking the Death Barrier." *Newsweek*, 19 February, 72.

Labaton, Stephen. 1994. "U.S. Judges Can Delay Executions to Allow Habeas Reviews, Justices Rule." *New York Times*, 1 July, A9.

_____. 1996. "New Habeas Corpus Law Is Constitutional, Both Sides Agree." *New York Times*, 4 June (from New York Times World Wide Web site: www.nytimes.com).

Lacayo, Richard. 1992. "You Don't Always Get Perry Mason." *Time*, 1 June, 38.

Lewis, Neil A. 1990. "Nominee's Replies on Court's Role Bring Questions." *New York Times*, 18 September, B7.

Loven, Jennifer. 1996. "Fed Oversight May End at Prisons." *Lansing State Journal*, 12 June, 3B.

Macedo, Stephen. 1987. *The New Right v. the Constitution*. Washington, DC: The Cato Institute.

Maguire, Kathleen and Ann L. Pastore, eds. 1996. *Sourcebook of Criminal Justice Statistics*. Washington, DC: U.S. Bureau of Justice Statistics.

Mandela, Nelson. 1994. *Long Walk to Freedom*. Boston: Little, Brown.

Marcus, Ruth. 1990. "Waiting Forever on Death Row." *Washington Post National Weekly Edition* 18 June, 12.

_____. 1991. "Haven't We Met Before?" *Washington Post National Weekly Edition*, 23-29 September, 14.

McCloskey, Robert G. 1994. *The American Supreme Court*, 2nd ed. Chicago: University of Chicago Press.

Memorandum to the Conference from Justice Antonin Scalia in No. 84-6811--*McCleskey v. Kemp* of January 6, 1987. *McCleskey v. Kemp* File, Thurgood Marshall Papers, The Library of Congress, Washington, DC.

Mitchell, Garry. 1993. "Murder Convict Is Cleared, Released." *Akron Beacon Journal* 3 March, A10.

Morgan, Richard E. 1984. *Disabling America: The "Rights Industry" in Our Time*. New York: Basic Books.

Mushlin, Michael. 1993. *Rights of Prisoners*, 2nd ed. Colorado Springs, CO: Shepard's/McGraw-Hill.

Nakell, Barry and Kenneth A. Hardy. 1987. *The Arbitrariness of the Death Penalty*. Philadelphia: Temple University Press.

"New Antiterrorism Law Contains Habeas Reform and Victim Restitution." 1996. *The Third Branch* 28 (May): 4.

"New Law Brings Broad Reforms to Prisoner Litigation." 1996. *The Third Branch* 28 (June): 3-6.

O'Brien, David. 1990. *Storm Center: The Supreme Court in American Life*, 2nd ed. New York: W.W. Norton.

O'Connor, Sandra Day. 1981. "Trends in the Relationship Between the Federal and State Courts from the Perspective of a State Court Judge." *William and Mary Law Review* 22: 801-815.

Popeo, Daniel J. and George C. Smith. 1987. "Court Supervision of Prisons Is Unnecessary." In *Criminal Justice Sources*, vol. 2. St. Paul, MN: Greenhaven Press.

Radelet, Michael L., Hugo Adam Bedeau, and Constance E. Putnam. 1992. *In Spite of Innocence: Erroneous Convictions in Capital Cases*. Boston: Northeastern University Press.

"Recent Cases, *Enmund v. Florida*, 102 S.Ct. 3368 (1982)." 1983. *New England Journal of Civil and Criminal Confinement* 9: 291-302.

Rehnquist, William H. 1987. *The Supreme Court: How It Was, How It Is*. New York: William Morrow.

_____. 1989. Interview in film *This Honorable Court* (PBS television broadcast), 12 September.

_____. 1992. "Chief Justice's 1991 Year-End Report on the Federal Judiciary." *The Third Branch* 24 (January): 1-6.

Reinhardt, Stephen. 1992. "The Supreme Court, the Death Penalty, and the *Harris* Case." *Yale Law Journal* 102: 205-224.

Reuben, Richard C. 1996. "New Habeas Restrictions Challenged." *ABA Journal* 82 (July): 22, 25.

Rowan, Carl T. 1993. *Dream Makers, Dream Breakers*. Boston: Little, Brown.

Scalia, Antonin. 1989. "Originalism: The Lesser Evil." *Cincinnati Law Review* 57: 849-865.

Schultz, David A. and Christopher E. Smith. 1996. *The Jurisprudential Vision of Justice Antonin Scalia*. Lanham, MD: Rowman & Littlefield.

Segal, Jeffrey A. and Harold J. Spaeth. 1993. *The Supreme Court and the Attitudinal Model*. New York: Cambridge University Press.

Shapiro, David L. 1973. "Federal Habeas Corpus: A Study in Massachusetts." *Harvard Law Review* 87: 321-372.

Slotnick, Elliot E. and Jennifer Segal. 1994. "'The Supreme Court Decided Today...,' Or Did It?" *Judicature* 78: 89-95.

Smith, Christopher E. 1987. "Examining the Boundaries of *Bounds*: Prison Law Libraries and Access to the Courts." *Howard Law Journal* 30: 27-44.

_____. 1989. "Jurisprudential Politics and the Manipulation of History." *Western Journal of Black Studies* 13: 156-161.

_____. 1989-90. "'What If....': Critical Junctures on the Road to (In)Equality." *Thurgood Marshall Law Review* 15: 1-25.

_____. 1990a. "Justice Antonin Scalia and the Institutions of American Government." *Wake Forest Law Review* 25: 783-809.

_____. 1990b. "Police Professionalism and the Rights of Criminal Defendants." *Criminal Law Bulletin* 26: 155-166.

_____. 1990c. "The Supreme Court's Emerging Majority: Restraining the High Court or Transforming Its Role?" *Akron Law Review* 24: 393-421.

_____. 1992. "Supreme Court Surprise: Justice Anthony Kennedy's Move Toward Moderation." *Oklahoma Law Review* 45: 459-476.

_____. 1993a. "Black Muslims and the Development of Prisoners' Rights." *Journal of Black Studies* 24: 131-146.

_____. 1993b. *Courts, Politics, and the Judicial Process*. Chicago: Nelson-Hall.

_____. 1993c. *Justice Antonin Scalia and the Supreme Court's Conservative Moment*. Westport, CT: Praeger Publishers.

_____. 1995a. "The Constitution and Criminal Punishment: The Emerging Visions of Justices Scalia and Thomas." *Drake Law Review* 43: 593-613.

_____. 1995b. "Judicial Policy Making and Habeas Corpus Reform." *Criminal Justice Policy Review* 7: 91-114.

Smith, Christopher E., Joyce A. Baugh, and Thomas R. Hensley. 1995. "The First-Term Performance of Justic Stephen Breyer." *Judicature* 79: 74-79.

Smith, Christopher E., Joyce Ann Baugh, Thomas R. Hensley, and Scott Patrick Johnson. 1994. "The First-Term Performance of Justice Ruth Bader Ginsburg." *Judicature* 78: 74-80.

Smith, Christopher E. and Thomas R. Hensley. 1993. "Assessing the Conservatism of the Rehnquist Court." *Judicature* 77: 83-89.

Smith, Christopher E. and Scott P. Johnson. 1992. "Newcomer on the High Court: Justice David Souter and the Supreme Court's 1990 Term." *South Dakota Law Review* 37: 901-923.

Smith, Christopher E. and Avis Alexandria Jones. 1993. "The Rehnquist Court's Activism and the Risk of Injustice." *Connecticut Law Review* 26: 53-77.

Smolowe, Jill. 1993. "The Trials of a Public Defender." *Time*, 29 March, 48.

Smothers, Ronald. 1993. "A Shortage of Lawyers to Help the Condemned." *New York Times*, 4 June, A21.

"Statistics Reflect Active Year for the Judiciary." 1994. *The Third Branch* 26 (February): 4-5.

Streib, Victor L. 1989. "Juveniles' Attitudes Toward Their Impending Executions." In *Facing the Death Penalty*, ed. M. Radelet. Philadelphia: Temple University Press.

Sullivan, J. Thomas. 1993. "A Practical Guide to Recent Developments in Federal Habeas Corpus to Practicing Attorneys." *Arizona State Law Journal* 25: 317-347.

The Supreme Court at Work. 1990. Washington, DC: Congressional Quarterly Press.

"Supreme Mystery." 1991. *Newsweek*, 16 September, 18-30.

Tate, C. Neal. 1991. "Personal Attribute Models of the Voting Behavior of United States Supreme Court Justices: Liberalism in Civil Liberties and Economic Decisions, 1946-1978." *American Political Science Review* 75: 355-367.

Tate, C. Neal and Roger Handberg. 1991. "Time Binding and Theory Building in Personal Attribute Models of Supreme Court Voting Behavior, 1916-1988." *American Journal of Political Science* 35: 460-480.

Terry, Don. 1996. "After 18 Years in Prison, 3 Cleared of Murders." *New York Times*, 3 July, A8.

"Tests Clear Man Convicted of Rape-Murder." 1993. *Kent (Ohio) Record-Courier* (Associated Press Wire Service), 28 June, 2.

Thomas, Jim. 1989. "The 'Reality' of Prisoner Litigation: Repackaging the Data." *New England Journal of Criminal and Civil Confinement* 15: 27-53.

Torassa, Ulysses. 1993. "Public Defenders Do Little Public Defending." *Cleveland Plain Dealer*, 27 June, 3B.

Walker, Samuel. 1977. *A Critical History of Police Reform*. Lexington, MA: Lexington Books.

_____. 1984. "'Broken Windows' and Fractured History: The Use and Misuse of History in Recent Police Patrol Analysis." *Justice Quarterly* 1: 75-90.

_____. 1989. *Sense and Nonsense About Crime*, 2nd ed. Pacific Grove, CA: Brooks/Cole.

Walker, Thomas G. and Lee Epstein. 1993. *The Supreme Court of the United States*. New York: St. Martin's Press.

Wallace, Donald H. 1994. "The Eighth Amendment and Prison Deprivations: Historical Revisions." *Criminal Law Bulletin* 30: 5-29.

"Warren McCleskey Is Dead." 1991. *New York Times*, 29 September, E16.

Wasby, Stephen L. 1976. *Continuity and Change: From the Warren Court to the Burger Court*. Pacific Palisades, CA: Goodyear Publishing.

_____. 1988. *The Supreme Court in the Federal Judicial System*, 3rd ed. Chicago: Nelson-Hall.

Weisselberg, Charles D. 1990. "Evidentiary Hearings in Federal Habeas Corpus Cases." *Brigham Young University Law Review* (1990): 131-181.

White, G. Edward. 1982. *Earl Warren: A Public Life*. New York: Oxford University Press.

_____. 1988. *The American Judicial Tradition*, rev. ed. New York: Oxford University Press.

White, Welsh S. 1991. *The Death Penalty in the Nineties*. Ann Arbor, MI: University of Michigan Press.

Williams, Juan. 1987. *Eyes on the Prize: America's Civil Rights Years, 1954-1965*. New York: Viking.

Willwerth, James. 1993. "Invitation to an Execution." *Time*, 22 November, 46.

Wilson, James Q. 1983. *Thinking About Crime*, rev. ed. New York: Basic Books.

Wolfe, Christopher. 1986. *The Rise of Modern Judicial Review*. New York: Basic Books.

Yackle Larry W. 1989. *Reform and Regret: The Story of Federal Judicial Involvement in the Alabama Prison System*. New York: Oxford University Press.

_____. 1993. "The Habeas Hagioscope." *Southern California Law Review* 66: 2331-2431.

_____. 1994. "Form and Function in the Administration of Justice: The Bill of Rights and Federal Habeas Corpus." *University of Michigan Journal of Law Reform* 24: 685-732.

Cases Cited

Akron v. Akron Center for Reproductive Health, 462 U.S. 416 (1983)
Arave v. Creech, 507 U.S. 463 (1993)
Argersinger v. Hamlin, 407 U.S. 25 (1972)
Austin v. United States, 509 U.S. 602 (1993)
Bell v. Wolfish, 441 U.S. 520 (1979)
Bennis v. Michigan, 116 S.Ct. 994 (1996)
Bivens v. Six Unknown Named Agents of the Federal Bureau of Narcotics, 403 U.S. 388 (1971)
Blystone v. Pennsylvania, 494 U.S. 299 (1990)
Booth v. Maryland, 482 U.S. 496 (1987)
Bounds v. Smith, 430 U.S. 817 (1977)
Brown v. Board of Education, 347 U.S. 483 (1954)
Burger v. Kemp, 483 U.S. 776 (1987)
Butler v. McKellar, 494 U.S. 407 (1989)
Callins v. Collins, 114 S.Ct. 1127 (1994)
Caplin & Drysdale v. United States, 491 U.S. 617 (1989)
City of Richmond v. J.A. Croson Co., 488 U.S. 469 (1989)
Coleman v. Thompson, 501 U.S. 722 (1991)
Cooper v. Pate, 378 U.S. 546 (1964)
Coy v. Iowa, 487 U.S. 1012 (1988)
Dawson v. Delaware, 503 U.S. 159 (1992)
Dolan v. City of Tigard, 114 S.Ct. 2309 (1994)
Douglas v. California, 372 U.S. 353 (1963)
Duckworth v. Eagan, 492 U.S. 195 (1989)
Duncan v. Louisiana, 391 U.S. 145 (1968)
Employment Division of Oregon v. Smith, 494 U.S. 872 (1990)
Enmund v. Florida, 458 U.S. 782 (1982)
Escobedo v. Illinois, 378 U.S. 478 (1964)

Estelle v. Gamble, 429 U.S. 97 (1976)

Farmer v. Brennan, 114 S.Ct. 1970 (1994)

Felker v. Turpin (I), 116 S.Ct. 1588 (1996)

Felker v. Turpin (II), 116 S.Ct. 2333 (1996)

Fierro v. Gomez, 865 F. Supp. 1387 (N.D. Cal. 1994)

Fierro v. 'Gomez, 94-16775, 21 February 1996 (9th Cir.)

Ford v. Wainwright, 477 U.S. 399 (1985)

Furman v. Georgia, 408 U.S. 238 (1972)

Garcia v. San Antonio Metropolitan Transit Authority, 469 U.S. 528 (1985)

Gideon v. Wainwright, 372 U.S. 335 (1963)

Gomez v. United States District Court, 112 S.Ct. 1653 (1992)

Graham v. Collins, 506 U.S. 461 (1993)

Gregg v. Georgia, 428 U.S. 153 (1976)

Hamilton v. Schiro, 338 F. Supp. 1016 (E.D. La. 1970)

Harmelin v. Michigan, 501 U.S. 957 (1991)

Harris v. Vazquez, 503 U.S. 1000 (1992)

Helling v. McKinney, 509 U.S. 25 (1993)

Herrera v. Collins, 506 U.S. 390 (1993)

Hitchcock v. Dugger, 481 U.S. 393 (1987)

Holt v. Sarver, 309 F. Supp. 362 (E.D. Ark. 1970)

Hudson v. McMillian, 503 U.S. 1 (1992)

Hutto v. Finney, 437 U.S. 678 (1978)

Illinois v. Rodriguez, 497 U.S. 177 (1990)

In re Kemmler, 136 U.S. 436 (1890)

International Society for Krishna Consciousness v. Lee, 505 U.S. 672 (1992)

Johnson v. Avery, 393 U.S. 483 (1969)

Johnson v. Texas, 509 U.S. 350 (1993)

Jones v. North Carolina Prisoners' Labor Union, 433 U.S. 119 (1977)

Korematsu v. United States, 323 U.S. 214 (1944)

Lee v. Weisman, 505 U.S. 577 (1992)

Lewis v. Casey, 116 S.Ct. 2174 (1996)

Lockett v. Ohio, 438 U.S. 586 (1978)

Lockhart v. Fretwell, 506 U.S. 364 (1993)

Louisiana ex rel. Francis v. Resweber, 329 U.S. 459 (1947)

Lucas v. South Carolina Coastal Commission, 505 U.S. 1003 (1992)

Mapp v. Ohio, 367 U.S. 643 (1961)

Maynard v. Cartwright, 486 U.S. 356 (1988)

McCleskey v. Kemp, 481 U.S. 279 (1987)

McCleskey v. Zant, 499 U.S. 467 (1991)

McFarland v. Scott, 114 S.Ct. 2568 (1994)
McKoy v. North Carolina, 494 U.S. 433 (1990)
Metro Broadcasting Co. v. Federal Communication Commission, 497 U.S. 547 (1990)
Miranda v. Arizona, 384 U.S. 436 (1966)
Missouri v. Jenkins, 495 U.S. 33 (1990)
Monroe v. Pape, 365 U.S. 167 (1961)
Murray v. Giarratano, 492 U.S. 1 (1989)
New York v. Quarles, 467 U.S. 649 (1984)
Nix v. Williams, 467 U.S. 431 (1984)
O'Dell v. Thompson, 502 U.S. 955 (1991)
O'Lone v. Estate of Shabazz, 482 U.S. 342 (1987)
O'Neal v. McAninch, 115 S.Ct. 992 (1995)
O'Neil v. Vermont, 144 U.S. 323 (1892)
Patterson v. McLean Credit Union, 491 U.S. 164 (1989)
Payne v. Tennessee, 501 U.S. 808 (1991)
Penry v. Lynaugh, 492 U.S. 302 (1989)
Planned Parenthood v. Casey, 505 U.S. 833 (1992)
Plyler v. Doe, 457 U.S. 202 (1982)
Regents of the University of California v. Bakke, 438 U.S. 265 (1978)
Rhodes v. Chapman, 452 U.S. 337 (1981)
Robinson v. California, 370 U.S. 660 (1962)
Roe v. Wade, 410 U.S. 113 (1973)
Romano v. Oklahoma, 114 S.Ct. 2004 (1994)
Ross v. Moffitt, 417 U.S. 600 (1974)
Rummel v. Estelle, 445 U.S. 263 (1980)
Schlup v. Delo, 115 S.Ct. 851 (1995)
Scott v. Illinois, 440 U.S. 367 (1979)
Shaw v. Reno, 113 S.Ct. 2816 (1993)
Simmons v. South Carolina, 114 S.Ct. 2187 (1994)
Sochor v. Florida, 504 U.S. 527 (1992)
Solem v. Helm, 463 U.S. 277 (1983)
South Carolina v. Gathers, 490 U.S. 805 (1989)
Stanford v. Kentucky, 492 U.S. 361 (1989)
Strickland v. Washington, 466 U.S. 668 (1984)
Sumner v. Schuman, 483 U.S. 66 (1987)
Teague v. Lane, 489 U.S. 288 (1989)
Texas v. Johnson, 491 U.S. 397 (1989)
Thompson v. Oklahoma, 487 U.S. 815 (1988)
Tison v. Arizona, 481 U.S. 137 (1987)
Trop v. Dulles, 356 U.S. 86 (1958)

Tuilaepa v. California, 114 S.Ct. 2630 (1994)
United States v. Cronic, 466 U.S. 648 (1984)
United States v. Eichman, 496 U.S. 310 (1990)
United States v. Leon, 468 U.S. 897 (1984)
United States v. Lopez, 115 S.Ct. 1624 (1995)
United States v. Monsanto, 491 U.S. 600 (1989)
United States v. Nixon, 418 U.S. 683 (1974)
United States v. Wade, 388 U.S. 218 (1967)
Walton v. Arizona, 497 U.S. 639 (1990)
Wards Cove Packing Co. v. Atonio, 490 U.S. 642 (1989)
Weems v. United States, 217 U.S. 349 (1910)
Whitley v. Albers, 475 U.S. 312 (1986)
Wilkerson v. Utah, 99 U.S. 130 (1879)
Wilson v. Seiter, 501 U.S. 294 (1991)
Woodson v. North Carolina, 428 U.S. 280 (1976)

Index

abortion, 8, 21, 23-26, 34
Abraham, Henry, 19
access to the courts, right of,
    12, 106, 109, 112, 132
accomplice, 86, 89, 99
Acker, James, 79
"actual innocence," 124
Adams, Randall, 122
adversarial model, 101, 125
affirmative action, 19, 21-26,
    32
African-American, 22, 26, 44,
    75-76, 94
aggravating factors, 51, 73, 85,
    90-94, 97, 99, 105
AIDS, 65
*Akron v. Akron Center for
    Reproductive Health*, 21
American Bar Association, 21,
    112
American Civil Liberties Union,
    27
American College of Trial
    Lawyers, 21
Antiterrorism and Effective
    Death Penalty Act, 115
appeals, 101, 103

appellate courts, 105, 113.
    See also Supreme Court, U.S.
appointment of justices, 30.
    See also justices; presi-
    dential appointments
Arave v. Creech, 91
Argersinger v. Hamlin, 101
Arkansas prisons, 45-47, 56, 60

"baby boom," 14
bail, 56, 63
Baldus, David, 75
Baldus study, 75-79
Baum, Lawrence, 30
Bedeau, Hugo, 124
Bell v. Wolfish, 40-41
Bennis v. Michigan, 56
Berkson, Larry, 43
bias, 97-98. *See also* discrim-
    ination
bifurcated proceeding, 73-74,
    98-99. *See also* sentencing
    hearing
Bill of Rights, 3, 9, 12, 20, 33,
    50, 108. *See also* individual
    amendments by number

Bivens v. Six Unknown Named Agents of the Federal Bureau of Narcotics, 16
Black, Hugo, 12, 16, 35-36
Blackmun, Harry, 9, 16, 21, 24, 27-28, 34, 48, 55, 57, 67, 88, 91, 95-96, 99
Bloodworth, Kirk, 122
Blystone v. Pennsylvania, 90
Booth v. Maryland, 80-83, 93
Bounds v. Smith, 17
Bork, Robert, 4, 25
Brennan, William, 10, 12, 21-29, 35-37, 72-77, 81, 88, 91, 96, 99, 132
Breyer, Stephen, 21, 27, 99
Brigham, John, 4
Brown v. Board of Education, 19, 22, 130
Burger v. Kemp, 105
Burger, Warren, 9, 13-16, 21-24, 87-88
Burger Court, 8-10, 15-18, 23, 28-29, 40-41, 45, 49, 71-74, 86, 99, 101, 132-133
Bush, George, 8, 10, 14, 18, 25-26, 29, 31
Bush administration, 58, 108
Butler v. McKellar, 109, 123

Callins v. Collins, 96
Caminker, Evan, 119-20
Canada, 11
capital punishment. *See* death penalty
Caplin and Drysdale v. United States, 105
Carter, Jimmy, 27
certiorari, writ of, 96
Chemerinsky, Erwin, 119-20

chief justice, 9-10, 16, 33. *See also* individual chief justices by name
civil rights, 14-15
Civil Rights Act of 1991, 115
civil rights lawsuits, 32, 44-45, 61, 65-67, 114, 118. *See also* prison conditions
civil service, 35-36
Circuit Justice, 110-11
City of Richmond v. J.A. Croson Co., 19, 32
Cleveland, Ohio, 12
Clinton, Bill, 21, 27, 115
Coleman v. Thompson, 110, 124
Columbia University, 27
Commerce Clause, 33
composition of the U.S. Supreme Court, 6, 9-10, 15, 26-27, 81, 87, 98, 116. *See also* individual justices by name
confrontation, right of, 3, 25
Congress, U.S., 28, 59, 69-70, 73, 106, 108-9, 113-16, 133
Constitution, U.S., 3-5, 20, 24-25, 30, 48, 56, 64, 77, 93, 96, 108, 124. *See also* individual rights by name and amendments by number
constitutional amendments, 3. *See also* individual amendments by number
constitutional interpretation, 22, 25
Cook, Julian, 77
Cooper v. Pate, 44
Cornell University, 27
counsel, right to, 12, 16, 101-7, 129. *See also* Sixth Amendment
court-martial, 43

Cox Archibald, 13
Coy v. Iowa, 25
crime, 6, 14, 108, 131
crime control, 39, 108, 113,
    127
crime rates, 14, 37
criminal law, 3, 13, 83
cruel and unusual punish-
    ment, 5-6, 8, 40-44, 48-
    49, 59, 64, 86, 95, 118.
    See also death penalty;
    Eighth Amendment; prison
    conditions

Davis, Sue, 20, 33
Dawson v. Delaware, 90
death penalty, 8, 17, 20, 27,
    42, 46-47, 49-53, 71-111,
    115-22, 129
Decker, John, 8, 39, 107
defense attorney, 12, 18, 97,
    101-7. *See also* counsel,
    right to; Sixth Amendment
"deliberate indifference," 46,
    57-61, 65-67
Democrats, 15, 21, 24, 31
denationalization, 43
discretion, 72-73, 78, 86, 88-
    90, 94-98, 133
discrimination, 5, 10, 18, 72-
    73, 75-83, 88-89, 93, 96,
    98-99, 128
district judges, U.S., 40,
    103, 114, 118
DNA, 122-23
Dolan v. City of Tigard, 56
Dorin, Dennis, 79-80
double-bunking, 47-48, 58, 60
Douglas v. California, 101
Douglas, William O., 10, 12,
    28, 35, 73-74

Duckworth v. Eagan, 18
due process, 5, 12, 29-30,
    39-40, 45, 71-72, 91, 125
Duncan v. Louisiana, 12

Eighth Amendment, 5-6, 39-70,
    120, 129-30
Eisenhower, Dwight, 12, 21
elected officials, 94, 97,
    110
electric chair, 42, 57
*Employment Division of Oregon
    v. Smith*, 28, 55
en banc, 118
England, 52
Enmund v. Florida, 86-89
Epstein, Lee, 6, 72
equal protection, 76-78,
    93-94, 128, 132
erroneous convictions, 104,
    121-125
Escobedo v. Illinois, 23
Estelle v. Gamble, 45-47,
    57-58, 68
ethnic groups, 32
excessive fines, 56
executive branch, 4, 25, 31,
    50, 124, 127
exclusionary rule, 12, 16-17,
    20, 35. *See also* Fourth
    Amendment

Farmer v. Brennan, 66-69, 128
FBI, 123
federal courts, 32-33, 92, 108-
    9, 113, 130
federal judges, 8, 44-47, 69,
    108, 124. *See also* judges
federalism, 33, 111
Felker v. Turpin, 116
felony-murder, 86-88, 99

Fifth Amendment, 5, 39, 47, 101, 107, 111
Fierro v. Gomez, 121
fines, 3, 94, 101
First Amendment, 23, 59, 91, 132
Ford v. Wainwright, 85
Ford, Gerald, 28
Ford administration, 24
forfeiture, 56, 105
forensic experts, 103
Fortas, Abe, 12, 15-16, 35
Fourteenth Amendment, 5, 12, 33, 76
Fourth Amendment, 5, 39, 107. *See also* exclusionary rule
Framers of the Constitution, 3, 50, 52, 54, 63-64, 108
Friedelbaum, Stanley, 39
Friedman, Lawrence, 63
frivolous appeals, 120
Furman v. Georgia, 72, 74, 88, 94, 96-97

Garcia v. San Antonio Metropolitan Transit, 33
gas chamber, 117-21
gender equality, 27-28
Georgia's capital punishment system, 73-80, 93
Gibson, James, 30
Gideon v. Wainwright, 12, 101, 130-31
Ginsburg, Douglas, 25
Ginsburg, Ruth Bader, 21, 23, 26-27, 55, 99, 115

Goldwater, Barry, 18
Graham v. Collins, 96
Gregg v. Georgia, 17, 73-74, 90, 99
Gross, Samuel, 98
Gun-Free Schools Act, 33

habeas corpus, 3, 8, 106-17, 122-23, 129, 131, 133
Habeas Corpus Act, 108
habitual offender, 48, 129
Hamilton v. Schiro, 45
"hands-off" doctrine, 40-41, 64
Harlan, John, 16
Harmelin v. Michigan, 49-63, 68, 129
harmless error, 110
Harris v. Vazquez, 120
Harris, Robert Alton, 117-21
Harvard University, 18, 21, 23-25, 27
Helling v. McKinney, 65-69, 128
Henry, Patrick, 3
Herrera v. Collins, 124
Hitchcock v. Dugger, 91-92
Hoffmann, Joseph, 71, 109
Holt v. Sarver, 45
Howard University, 22
Hudson v. McMillian, 61-62, 68, 128
Hutto v. Finney, 46-47, 60

Illinois v. Rodriguez, 18
illiteracy, 106
impeachment, 28, 116
In re Kemler, 42

indigent defendants, 12-13, 104-06. *See also* counsel, right to
ineffective assistance of counsel, 102, 104, 110
inevitable discovery rule, 17
"injury in fact," 106
insanity, 85
International Society of Krishna Consciousness v. Lee, 59
interrogation. *See* questioning by police
Islam, 44

Jackson, Robert, 18
jail, 40, 45, 63, 66, 123
jailhouse lawyers, 106
Japanese-Americans, 30
Johnson, Lyndon, 15, 22
Johnson v. Avery, 12
Johnson v. Texas, 85, 95
Jones v. North Carolina Prisoners Labor Union, 132
judges, 4, 15, 31-32, 66, 72-74, 86, 89, 91-93, 117, 127, 133. *See also* federal judges; justices
judicial activism, 64, 116
Judicial Conference of the United States, 109
judicial decision making, 6, 8-11, 19, 29-34, 37, 41, 55, 89, 99, 128, 130, 133
judicial myth, 4
judicial restraint, 8, 20, 25, 31-34, 99, 110-17
judiciary, 24, 31, 69, 109, 113
Judiciary Committee, U.S. Senate, 20
jury, 5, 66, 72-74, 82-98, 110 110

Justice Department, U.S., 31
justices, U.S. Supreme Court, 6, 8, 27, 29, 113. *See also* individual justices by name
juveniles, 83-85, 99, 128

Kairys, David, 39
Kamisar, Yale, 17
Kende, Mark, 77
Kennedy, Anthony, 10, 23, 25, 27, 36, 50, 52, 64, 84
Kennedy, John F., 23
Kobylka, Joseph, 72
Korematsu v. United States, 30

law clerk, 19, 23
law enforcement. *See* police
law reform, 109-17, 129, 133. *See also* habeas corpus
law school, 29, 53
lawyers, 31, 35-36, 72, 103, 106, 119, 123
legal assistance in prison, 69
Legal Defense Fund (LDF), 72
legislative districts, 77
legislature, 4, 8, 19, 25, 31, 33, 43, 50, 69, 73, 108, 127. *See also* Congress
Lewis v. Casey, 69, 106
Library of Congress, 79
life sentence, 20, 48, 50-51, 129-30
line-ups, 102
Lockhart v. Fretwell, 105, 110
Lockett v. Ohio, 74, 95
Louisiana ex rel. Francis v. Resweber, 57-58
Lucas v. South Carolina Coastal Commission, 56

Macias, Federico Martinez, 104
magistrate judge, U.S., 113
mandatory sentences, 74, 90,
   95, 97-98, 129-30
Mapp v. Ohio, 12, 16-17, 35, 40
Marshall, Thurgood, 10, 12, 22-
   29, 36-37, 46, 55, 57, 72,
   74, 79, 82, 85, 88, 91,
   96, 99, 132-33
Maynard v. Cartwright, 91
McCleskey v. Kemp, 75-83, 93
McCleskey v. Zant, 106, 110,
   118
McCloskey, Robert, 4-5
McFarland v. Scott, 107
McKoy v. North Carolina, 95
McKenna, Joseph, 42
McMillian, Walter, 122
medical care in prison, 46,
   49, 60, 65, 68
*Metro Broadcasting Co. v.
   Federal Communication
   Commission*, 22
mental illness, 106
mental retardation, 83, 84, 86,
   95, 99, 123, 128
Miranda v. Arizona, 12, 16, 18,
   23, 26, 35, 40, 102
Missouri v. Jenkins, 22, 25
mitigating factors, 51, 73-74,
   82-85, 90-99, 104
Monroe v. Pape, 44
Murray v. Giarratano, 106
Michael Mushlin, 130

NAACP, 22
Nationality Act of 1940, 43
New York v. Quarles, 17, 28
New York Times, 109, 122
news media, 131
Ninth Circuit, 117-21

Nix v. Williams, 17
Nixon, Richard, 14-16, 19-23,
   31, 116
Northwestern University, 27

objective standard, 47-48, 58,
   60, 62, 66
O'Brien, David, 130
O'Connor, Sandra, 9-10, 21, 27-
   29, 31, 33, 36, 50, 52, 62,
   64, 69, 84-85, 87-89, 112
O'Dell v. Thompson, 123
O'Lone v. Shabazz, 130
O'Neal v. McAninch, 125
O'Neil v. Vermont, 42
opinion assignment, 9, 51
oral argument, 115
original intent, 50, 52, 54,
   63, 66, 95
Oxford University, 23, 25

*Patterson v. McLean Credit
   Union*, 19
Payne v. Tennessee, 82-83, 93
Penry v. Lynaugh, 85-86, 95-96
plea bargain, 97-98
Planned Parenthood v. Casey,
   8
Plyler v. Doe, 21
police, 5, 8, 12-18, 26, 32,
   35-36, 44, 107, 110, 123-
   24, 127, 133
police misconduct, 14, 17, 35-
   36, 49
political parties, 31, 34, 108
political patronage, 103
politicians, 12, 35, 131
Powell, Lewis, 16, 21, 23, 25,
   31, 48, 75-80, 87, 109
precedent, 10, 20, 22, 29, 51,
   53, 55, 60, 81-82, 130

presidential appointments, 6, 8, 15-16, 31

president, 6, 39-40. *See also* individual presidents by name

prison administration, 40-41

prison conditions, 5, 40-41, 46-49, 57-70, 128, 130. *See also* civil rights lawsuits; cruel and unusual punishment; Eighth Amendment

prison law library, 69-70, 106, 133

Prison Litigation Reform Act of 1996, 69

prison officials, 5, 12, 44, 48, 58, 61-65, 130, 133

prison population, 11, 133

prison reform, 69-70, 133

prisons, 8, 12, 16, 44-45, 61, 64, 66

property rights, 56

probation, 3

professionalism, 35-37, 69, 133

proportionality, 40, 42-43, 47-56, 59, 61, 68, 86, 129-30

prosecutors, 4-5, 31, 35, 83, 89, 97-98, 103, 107, 124, 127-28, 133

public defender, 103. *See also* defense attorney

public opinion, 72, 130-32

public policy, 4-5, 8, 16-17, 31-32, 72, 94, 104

"public safety" exception, 17

Pulaski, Charles, 75

punishment, defined, 58, 66, 95

Putnam, Constance, 124

racial minority, 19, 32, 75, 110. *See also* discrimination

racial segregation, 30, 130-31

Radelet, Michael, 124

Reagan, Ronald, 8, 10, 14, 18, 24-25, 28-29, 31

Reagan administration, 108

"reckless indifference," 88-89

Regents of the University of California v. Bakke, 19, 21

Rehnquist, William, 9-10, 16-21, 24, 27-33, 36, 41, 47, 50-51, 56, 64, 69, 82, 84, 87, 109-12, 124-25

Rehnquist Court's uniqueness, 8-11

Reinhardt, Stephen, 117, 119-20

religion, freedom of, 44

Republicans, 6, 9, 15, 21, 27-28, 31, 34, 39

retroactivity, 14, 32, 110, 123

Rhodes v. Chapman, 17, 48, 58, 60

Richardson, James, 121

rights, 4-14, 17-18, 31, 35, 39, 58, 64-65, 107, 112-16, 123, 127-33. *See also* individual rights by name and amendments by number

Robinson v. California, 41, 44

Roe v. Wade, 24, 34

Romano v. Oklahoma, 91

Ross v. Moffitt, 101

Rummell v. Estelle, 20, 48

Rutgers University, 26

Rutledge, Wiley, 27

questioning by police, 5, 36, 98, 101, 123

Scalia, Antonin, 4, 10, 24-28, 31-36, 40, 50-69, 79-84, 87-88, 92-99, 111, 124, 129
Schlup v. Delo, 125
school desegregation, 18, 22
Scott v. Illinois, 101
search and seizure, 5, 12, 36, 39. *See also* Fourth Amendment; exclusionary rule
self-incrimination, 101. *See also* Fifth Amendment; questioning by police
Senate, U.S., 15, 20, 25-27
sentencing, 11, 128
sentencing hearing, 80-82, 104. *See also* bifurcated proceeding
sexual harassment, 26
Shaw v. Reno, 77
"significant injury," 62, 68, 128
Simmons v. South Carolina, 91
Simpson, O.J., 103
Sixth Amendment, 3, 12, 39, 101, 107, 129. *See also* counsel, right to
Sochor v. Florida, 95, 128
social class, 83
social science, 14, 30, 75-76, 79, 99, 111-12
Solem v. Helm, 48, 51, 130
Solicitor General of the United States, 22
South Africa, 72
Soviet Union, 71-72
Souter, David, 10, 23, 25-27, 31, 36, 50, 52, 67, 81-82, 115
South Carolina v. Gathers, 81-82

speedy trial, 3, 16
Stanford University, 18, 28
Stanford v. Kentucky, 84
stare decisis, 51, 95
state constitutions, 41, 43
state courts, 12-13, 28, 33, 41-42, 111-12, 132
state government, 32, 41, 92, 104
state judges, 43, 110
state legislatures, 11, 13, 20, 28, 48, 60, 90, 97
state supreme court, 72
statistical proof, 75-81, 93, 128
statutory interpretation, 19, 25
Stevens, John Paul, 9, 24, 26-29, 67-68, 82, 88, 91, 106, 115
Stewart, Potter, 28, 35, 44, 73-74
stop and frisk, 14
Strickland v. Washington, 102
Streib, Victor, 84
subjective standard, 46-47, 49, 58, 60, 67-69, 128, 130
Sullivan, J. Thomas, 112
Sumner v. Schumer, 90
Supreme Court, U.S., 4-6, 9, 22, 79, 109, 127, 130, 132. *See also* individual justices by name
symbolism, 3, 22, 24, 40, 49, 104, 106, 127, 129

Teague v. Lane, 109
Texas v. Johnson, 25
The Thin Blue Line, 122

Thomas, Clarence, 10, 23, 27, 31, 33, 40, 55-56, 63-69, 85, 91-99
Thomas, Jim, 111
Thompson v. Oklahoma, 83
Thornberry, Homer, 15
"three-strikes" laws, 129. *See also* habitual offender; mandatory sentences
Tison v. Arizona, 75, 87-89
tobacco smoke in prison, 65, 128
torture, 47, 64
"totality of circumstances," 60
trial, 93, 97, 109
trial by jury, 12, 91
Trop v. Dulles, 43, 46, 54, 117
Tuilaepa v. California, 99
United States v. Cronic, 102
United States v. Eichman, 25
United States v. Leon, 17
United States v. Monsanto, 105
United States v. Nixon, 116
United States v. Wade, 102
University of Chicago, 24
University of Colorado, 23
University of Virginia, 24

Virginia State Board of Education, 21
Vinson, Fred, 22
Victim Impact Statements, 80, 82, 93

Walker, Thomas, 6
Walton v. Arizona, 91, 94-95
Wards Cove Packing Co. v. Atonio, 10, 19
warrantless search, 18
Warren, Earl, 6, 12, 15, 21-22, 35

Warren Court, 6, 8-9, 12-14, 16-23, 26, 36-37, 40, 43-45, 49, 130, 133
Wasby, Stephen, 17
Washington and Lee University, 21
Washington Post, 123
Watergate, 116
Weisselberg, Charles, 111
Weems v. United States, 42-43, 53
White, Byron, 21, 23, 27, 29, 31, 55, 57, 60-61, 64-65, 73, 84, 86, 88-89, 110-11
White, G. Edward, 10
Whitley v. Albers, 49, 58
Whittaker, Charles, 23
Wickersham Commission, 35-36
Wilkerson v. Utah, 42
Wilson v. Seiter, 49, 57-64, 66-69, 130
Wolfe, Christopher, 13
World War II, 18, 30, 43, 94
Woodson v. North Carolina, 74, 90, 94-95
Woodworth, George, 75

Yackle, Larry, 108, 113, 129
Yale University, 23, 26